Longman Exam Guides

ACCOUNTING STANDARDS

Geoff Black

LONGMAN
London and New York

Longman Group UK Limited
Longman House, Burnt Mill, Harlow
Essex CM20 2JE, England
and Associated Companies throughout the world

Published in the United States of America
by Longman Inc., New York

First published 1987

British Library Cataloguing in Publication Data
Black, Geoff
   Accounting standards.——(Longman exam guides)
   1. Accounting——Standards
   I. Title
657'.0218   HF5657
ISBN 0-582-46923-6

Library of Congress Cataloguing-in-Publication Data
Black, Geoff
   Accounting standards.

   (Longman exam guides)
   Includes index.
   1. Accounting——Examinations, questions, etc.
I. Title   II. Series.
HF5661.B57   1987   657'.076   86–20963
ISBN 0–582–46923–6

Set in 9½ on 11pt Linotron Times
Printed and bound in Great Britain at
The Bath Press, Avon

Longman Exam Guides
Accounting Standards

Longman Exam Guides

Series Editors: Stuart Wall and David Weigall

Titles available:

Accounting Standards
Bookkeeping and Accounting
British Government and Politics
Business Law
Economics
English as a Foreign Language: Intermediate
English Literature
French
Monetary Economics
Office Practice and Secretarial Administration
Pure Mathematics
Quantitative Methods
Secretarial Skills

Forthcoming:

Accounting: Cost and Management
             Financial
Biology
Business Communication
Business Studies
Chemistry
Commerce
Computer Science
Electronics
Elements of Banking
English as a Foreign Language: Advanced
English as a Foreign Language: Preliminary
General Principles of Law
General Studies
Geography
Mechanics
Modern British History
Physics
Sociology
Taxation

Contents

Editors' Preface

Much has been said in recent years about declining standards and disappointing examination results. Whilst this may be somewhat exaggerated, examiners are well aware that the performance of many candidates falls well short of their potential. Longman Exam Guides are written by experienced examiners and teachers, and aim to give you the best possible foundation for examination success. There is no attempt to cut corners. The books encourage thorough study and a full understanding of the concepts involved and should be seen as course companions and study guides to be used throughout the year. Examiners are in no doubt that a structured approach in preparing for and taking examinations can, together with hard work and diligent application, substantially improve performance.

The largely self-contained nature of each chapter gives the book a useful degree of flexibility. After starting with Chapters 1 and 2, all other chapters can be read selectively, in any order appropriate to the stage you have reached in your course. We believe that this book, and the series as a whole, will help you establish a solid platform of basic knowledge and examination technique on which to build.

Stuart Wall and David Weigall

Acknowledgements

The Accounting Standards Committee has kindly given me its permission to reproduce extracts from Statements of Standard Accounting Practice.

I am also indebted to the following examination boards and professional bodies for allowing me permission to reproduce past examination questions:

Association of Accounting Technicians; Certified Diploma in Accounting and Finance; Chartered Association of Certified Accountants; Institute of Bankers; Institute of Chartered Accountants in England and Wales; Institute of Chartered Secretaries and Administrators; Institute of Cost and Management Accountants; London Chamber of Commerce and Industry; University of London Schools Examinations Board.

The University of London Schools Examinations Board accepts no responsibility whatsoever for the accuracy or method of working in the answers given.

I am also grateful to the following companies who have allowed me to use extracts from their published annual reports; ASDA-MFI Group plc, Associated British Foods plc, Bardon Hill Group plc, Bryant Holdings plc, The Boots Company plc, DRG plc, Exco International plc, Glynwed plc, Foseco-Minsep plc, Grand Metropolitan plc, Guiness plc, Laing Properties plc, Ladbroke Group plc, Marks and Spencer plc, J. Sainsbury plc, Storehouse plc, Tate and Lyle plc, Tarmac Construction plc, TV-am plc, and United Biscuits plc.

My thanks go to my father, Robert Black, for help in reviewing material and for his much valued advice. I would also like to express my thanks to my wife for her constant encouragement and help.

Thanks also to John Blake and Stuart Wall for their advice and comments and to Brian Hodgkinson of CCAT for help in obtaining information.

Geoff Black
Cambridge
1986

To Rachel, Susannah and Andrew

Chapter 1

The examinations

Since 1971, Statements of Standard Accounting Practice (SSAPs) have become essential materials for both professional accountants and students, and *every* examination in financial accounting (as opposed to bookkeeping) is likely to require some knowledge of several standards.

The depth of understanding will vary, of course, depending upon the syllabus content of the particular examination. The intention of this book is to cover the main requirements of every standard at levels which are appropriate for both 'intermediate' and 'final' level students. The latter category may well need to undertake further research and background reading, particularly in the area of *exposure drafts* and *International Accounting Standards*. For this purpose, there is a section at the end of each chapter which contains references to other texts.

In addition to being suitable for the examinations of the professional accountancy bodies, this book is also appropriate for LCCI, A level, AAT and equivalent courses, as well BTEC Higher Level qualifications. A guide to syllabus coverage is given on pages 2 to 5, which indicates the extent to which syllabuses refer to specific standards. Students are recommended to read the actual syllabuses for information regarding the depth of knowledge required for their own course.

Readers are advised to keep abreast of developments relating to SSAPs, as there is continuing activity in regard to the revision of existing standards and the creation of new ones. It helps to read the professional press, including *Accountancy* as well as magazines such as *Pass* and *Certified Accountants Students Newsletter*. Many public libraries stock some of these titles.

The full text of the standards is obtainable from the publications department of any of the major accountancy bodies. The address of one of these is: The Institute of Chartered Accountants in England and Wales (ICAEW), Gloucester House, 399, Silbury Boulevard, Witan Gate East, Central Milton Keynes, MK9 2HL.

SYLLABUS COVERAGE CHART

SYLLABUS CHAPTER	ICMA Cost a/c	ICMA Fin a/c	ICMA Adv Fin a/c	ICAEW Fin a/c 1	ICAEW Fin a/c 2	ACCA Reg. Fwk	ACCA AAP
4. Accounting Policies		✓	✓	✓	✓	✓	✓
5. Government Grants		✓	✓	✓	✓	✓	✓
Depreciation		✓	✓	✓	✓	✓	✓
Investment Properties		✓	✓	✓	✓	✓	✓
6. Research and Development	✓	✓	✓	✓	✓	✓	✓
H P and Leasing		✓	✓		✓	✓	✓
Goodwill		✓	✓	✓	✓	✓	✓
7. Stocks and WIP	✓	✓	✓	✓	✓	✓	✓
8. Funds Flow		✓	✓	✓	✓	✓	✓
9. VAT		✓	✓	✓	✓	✓	✓
Imputation System		✓	✓	✓	✓	✓	✓
Deferred Tax		✓	✓		✓	✓	✓
10. Earnings per Share		✓	✓		✓	✓	✓
Extraordinary Items		✓	✓	✓	✓	✓	✓
11. Post Balance Sheet Events		✓	✓	✓	✓	✓	✓
Contingencies		✓	✓	✓	✓	✓	✓
12. Associated Companies			✓	✓	✓	✓	✓
Groups of Companies		✓	✓	✓	✓	✓	✓
Mergers and Acquisitions			✓	✓	✓	✓	✓
13. Foreign Currency			✓	✓	✓	✓	✓
Appendix			✓		✓	✓	✓
Current Cost Accounting							

ICMA– Institute of Cost and Management Accountants
ICAEW–Institute of Chartered Accountants in England and Wales
ACCA– Chartered Association of Certified Accountants
ICSA– Institute of Chartered Secretaries and Administrators
AAT– Association of Accounting Technicians

ACCA	ICSA	AAT	IOB	GCE	LCCI	RSA	AIA
Adv Fin a/c	Fin a/c	Fin a/c	Acctcy	A Level	Higher	III	Fin a/c II & III
✓	✓	✓	✓	✓	✓	✓	✓
✓	✓	✓		✓			✓
✓	✓	✓	✓	✓	✓	✓	✓
✓	✓	✓					✓
✓	✓	✓	✓	✓	✓		✓
✓	✓	✓					✓
✓	✓	✓	✓	✓			✓
✓	✓	✓	✓	✓	✓	✓	✓
✓	✓	✓	✓	✓	✓	✓	✓
✓	✓	✓		✓		✓	✓
✓	✓	✓	✓	✓			✓
✓	✓	✓	✓				✓
✓	✓	✓		✓			✓
✓	✓	✓	✓	✓	✓	✓	✓
✓	✓	✓		✓			✓
✓	✓	✓		✓			✓
✓	✓	✓	✓	✓			✓
✓	✓	✓	✓	✓	✓		✓
✓	✓	✓	✓				✓
✓	✓	✓					✓
✓	✓	✓	✓	✓			✓

IOB–	Institute of Bankers
LCCI–	London Chamber of Commerce and Industry
RSA–	Royal Society of Arts
AIA–	Association of International Accountants

SYLLABUS COVERAGE CHART

CHAPTER	SYLLABUS ACEA Adv a/c	IAA Acctg 3	IAA Adv a/c	SCCA Fin a/c*	SCCA Co a/c*	SCCA Fin a/c 1†	SCCA Fin a/c 2†
4. Accounting Policies	✓	✓	✓	✓	✓	✓	✓
5. Government Grants	✓	✓	✓	✓	✓	✓	✓
Depreciation	✓	✓	✓	✓	✓	✓	✓
Investment Properties	✓	✓	✓	✓	✓	✓	
6. Research and Development	✓	✓	✓	✓	✓	✓	✓
H P and Leasing	✓	✓	✓	✓	✓		
Goodwill	✓	✓	✓	✓	✓	✓	✓
7. Stocks and WIP	✓	✓	✓	✓	✓	✓	✓
8. Funds Flow	✓	✓	✓	✓	✓	✓	✓
9. VAT	✓	✓	✓		✓		✓
Imputation System	✓	✓	✓		✓		✓
Deferred Tax	✓	✓	✓		✓		
10. Earnings per Share	✓	✓	✓		✓		✓
Extraordinary Items	✓	✓	✓	✓	✓	✓	✓
11. Post Balance Sheet Events	✓	✓	✓	✓	✓		✓
Contingencies	✓	✓	✓	✓	✓		✓
12. Associated Companies	✓	✓	✓	✓	✓		
Groups of Companies	✓	✓	✓	✓	✓		
Mergers and Acquisitions	✓	✓	✓	✓	✓		
13. Foreign Currency	✓	✓	✓	✓	✓		
Appendix	✓	✓	✓		✓		
Current Cost Accounting							

ACEA– Association of Cost and Executive Accountants

IAA– Institute of Administrative Accountants

SCCA– Society of Company and Commercial Accountants

ABE– Association of Business Executives

ICAS– Institute of Chartered Accountants of Scotland

* Examinable until end of 1988.

† Examinable from November 1987.

| SCCA | ABE | ICAS | ICAI | ICPAI | CIPFA | BTEC(H) | SCOTVEC | Univ, | DMS |
Fin a/c 3†	A/c & Fin								
✓	✓	✓	✓	✓	✓	✓	✓	✓	✓
✓		✓	✓	✓	✓	✓	✓	✓	✓
✓	✓	✓	✓	✓	✓	✓	✓	✓	✓
✓	✓	✓	✓	✓	✓	✓	✓	✓	✓
✓	✓	✓	✓	✓	✓	✓	✓	✓	✓
✓	✓	✓	✓	✓	✓	✓	✓	✓	✓
✓	✓	✓	✓	✓	✓	✓	✓	✓	✓
✓	✓	✓	✓	✓	✓	✓	✓	✓	✓
✓	✓	✓	✓	✓	✓	✓	✓	✓	✓
✓	✓	✓	✓	✓	✓	✓	✓	✓	✓
✓	✓	✓	✓	✓	✓	✓	✓	✓	✓
✓	✓	✓	✓	✓	✓	✓	✓	✓	✓
✓		✓	✓	✓	✓	✓	✓	✓	✓
✓		✓	✓	✓	✓	✓	✓	✓	✓
✓		✓	✓	✓	✓	✓	✓	✓	✓
✓		✓	✓	✓	✓	✓	✓	✓	✓
✓		✓	✓	✓	✓	✓	✓	✓	✓
✓	✓	✓	✓	✓	✓	✓	✓	✓	✓
✓		✓	✓	✓	✓	✓	✓	✓	✓
✓		✓	✓	✓	✓	✓	✓	✓	✓
✓		✓	✓	✓	✓	✓	✓	✓	✓

BTEC–   Business and Technician Education Council (Higher)
SCOTVEC– Scottish Vocational Educational Council
ICPAI–   Institute of Certified Public Accountants of Ireland
CIPFA–   Chartered Institute of Public Finance and Accountancy
Univ.–   University Accountancy Degree Courses
DMS–   Diploma in Management Studies
ICAI–   Institute of Chartered Accountants in Ireland

Chapter 2

Examination techniques

The golden rule concerning examination techniques is that there is no golden rule. Each examination candidate is an individual whose approach must allow for different circumstances and attitudes. What is certain, however, is that the candidates who pace their work at a steady rate throughout their course have a far better chance of gaining success than those who leave their efforts until the last moment. With this principle in mind, the following represents a breakdown of the major time divisions of a study course. Whilst geared primarily to college-based tuition. It is applicable in many respects to other learning methods, such as correspondence courses.

PRIOR TO THE COURSE

If you are studying for the examinations of a professional body, ensure firstly that you are registered as a student, and check on the availability of exemptions for any prior qualifications which you possess. If you are an employee, enquire as to the possibility of obtaining 'day release' to attend courses, and in any event, see if your employer is prepared to pay all or part of your fees and textbook costs. Do not be tempted to buy second-hand textbooks; they are invariably out of date and useless for studying accounting standards, as standards tend to be revised at regular intervals.

The courses at many colleges are over-subscribed, so it is best to enrol at the earliest opportunity. Do make use of college facilities; most colleges have an accommodation officer to help full-time students to find 'digs', and there are other people available to sort out grant queries, or advise on facilities for disabled students. They are there to help, so do not be afraid to contact them.

DURING THE COURSE

Complete the work at a steady pace, and endeavour to hand work in on time. Explain to your lecturer if you are unable to meet deadlines;

he may be sympathetic! Be prepared to ask questions, either during the lecture or informally after the lecture. Do not 'suffer in silence' as this does you no good, and may lead the lecturer to believe that you do not need any help. If there are personal problems which are disrupting your study pattern, seek help from the college student counselling service, or discuss them with friends or relations.

Get into the habit of reading a quality newspaper. This will help you to keep abreast of current affairs and appreciate good literary styles, which will be useful when you need to compose your own essays.

Many students find it useful to make their own notes of each topic as they progress through the course. This serves to reinforce the learning process and provides excellent revision material when used in conjunction with this book.

THE REVISION PERIOD

Revision is often undertaken in a haphazard way, when it should be approached in a logical and structured manner, particularly when the student has to take several examinations. One way of achieving this is to prepare a revision planner, which sets out the work to be covered and the dates available. The planner should incorporate some leisure activities, and be reasonably flexible. For example, there is no point in *forcing* yourself to work when you are over-tired. It is more beneficial to have a good night's sleep!

As the examination date draws near, establish the precise location of the exam hall, and make all necessary travel preparations. Check on writing materials, calculator and batteries, watch, lucky charms, etc. Make an 'exam pack' to keep them all together. Include any official exam entry documents, if required.

On the day before the examination, spend some time in reading through your notes. Get to bed early, and *set an alarm clock*!

THE DAY OF THE EXAMINATION

Have your usual breakfast, and choose clothes which are comfortable, and loose-fitting. Find your 'exam pack', and leave for the examination hall in good time, allowing for events such as traffic delays.

If you have exams in both morning and afternoon sessions, do not be tempted to drink alcohol with your lunch, for obvious reasons.

THE EXAMINATION

If you are allowed to choose your position in the hall, find a location which is well lit (but not in the full glare of the sun). Avoid desks which are next to radiators or the entrance doors.

Read the rubric carefully. If you are allowed reading time (e.g. IOB Accountancy), make the most of this by reading carefully through the paper, locating the first question which you wish to attempt. If, as is more likely, there is no specific reading time allowed, you should commence by confirming the number of questions to be answered from each section. Read through the paper and identify a question on a topic on which you feel confident. Be careful to allocate the time available. In a three-hour exam, a rough guide is 1.7 minutes per mark. This allows 10 minutes for reading, etc.

When answering a question, use rough notes to marshal your facts, before drawing them together in your answer. Avoid 'waffle': the best answers are those which are concise and relevant (see 'Answers' at the end of each chapter). If you are short of time, write your answer in note form.

Be as neat as possible; remember that an examiner has to read your answer, and is unlikely to be impressed with untidy work. Any 'workings' should be clearly marked as such, and rough work should be struck through after completion. It is particularly important to submit your workings with your answer, as they often provide additional information to the examiner on which extra marks can be awarded.

Take care with your choice of language, avoiding personal pronouns (e.g. 'I think that . . .') and prejudices (e.g. 'Profit-making is immoral').

Never waste time in writing out the question at the head of your answer, there are no marks to be gained by this. Keep the use of abbreviations to a minimum, and in any case only use those which are likely to be readily understood by the examiner, e.g. SSAP, P&L a/c.

Use the full time allocation allowed and do not be tempted to leave the exam hall early. If you have completed the required number of questions with time to spare, go back to the beginning of your answers, correcting errors and generally reviewing your work. Remember that even one extra mark gained in this way could mean the difference between success and failure.

AFTER THE EXAMINATION

Once the examination is over, it is better not to indulge in a 'post-mortem', as it may only serve to depress you when you compare your own answers with the textbook. Gain comfort from the fact that you do not need 100 per cent to pass. So long as you have given the examiner reasonably precise answers to the required number of questions, then success should be yours.

What are standards?

Chapter 3

A GETTING STARTED

The first Statement of Standard Accounting Practice (SSAP) was issued in 1970. In the preceding decade, the accountancy profession had been coming under increasing pressure to impose standardised procedures upon its members, to avoid inconsistencies between companies and to improve generally the quality and usefulness of the financial statements. One particular factor which brought demands for action from both accountants and non-accountants was a number of highly publicised cases where companies and individuals, having relied upon the work of professional accountants for takeover or investment decisions, found subsequently that valuations, etc. had been made on the basis of unsound or inconsistent accounting treatments. For example, in 1967, Associated Electrical Industries Ltd (AEI) was taken over by the General Electric Company Ltd (GEC) after a hotly contested bid. AEI had forecast a profit of £10 m for 1967, and GEC had based its bid price partly on this forecast. The bid was successful, but when the actual results for AEI were announced, a *loss* of £4.5 m was reported. The former auditors of AEI defended themselves by issuing a statement saying that AEI attributed

'. . . roughly £5 m to adverse differences which are matters substantially of fact rather than judgement and the balance of some £9.5 m to adjustments which remain substantially matters of judgement'.

The accounting policies adopted by AEI were perfectly acceptable at the time, but from the point of view of the general public, such diversity of accounting practice brings the accountancy profession as a whole into disrepute. SSAPs have been welcomed both by preparers and users of the financial statements, as ways of narrowing the areas of individuality available to accountants. Despite specific areas of difficulty, particularly in the field of accounting for inflation, SSAPs are likely to remain of value for many years to come.

B ESSENTIAL PRINCIPLES

THE STANDARD-SETTING PROCESS

The standard-setting process is performed in the UK by the **Accounting Standards Committee** (ASC), which is a subcommittee of the Consultative Committee of Accountancy Bodies (CCAB). The CCAB links the six major accountancy bodies for the purpose of co-ordinating various professional activities. The ASC is comprised of delegates from the six CCAB bodies, as well as non-accountant members who represent the interests of users, and of the government. The objectives of the standard-setting process were laid down in a paper issued in 1969 by the Institute of Chartered Accountants in England and Wales, entitled *A Statement of Intent on Accounting Standards in the 1970's*. They were:

1. To narrow the areas of difference and variety in accounting;
2. To recommend disclosure of accounting bases;
3. To require disclosure of departure from standards;
4. To introduce a system for wide consultation on standard setting;
5. To seek improvements in existing disclosure requirements of company law and the Stock Exchange.

In the main, these objectives have been met, and the impact of SSAPs will be obvious to anyone who reads through a company's financial statements. As readers progress through this book, they will become aware of the requirements of individual statements. Each of these serves to encourage accountants not only to apply consistent accounting procedures where appropriate, but also to *disclose* the policies which have been adopted, or disclose instances where standards have not been complied with.

In 1983, the ASC issued a report which followed a review of the standard-setting process. Its main conclusions were:

(a) Future accounting standards should deal only with matters of major and fundamental importance affecting the generality of companies. They will therefore be few in number.

(b) Statements of Recommended Practice (SORPs) were to be introduced, to cover matters which, whilst not meeting the criteria laid down in (a) above, still required authoritative pronouncements by the ASC to aid the development of accounting thought. SORPs are not mandatory on members of the accountancy profession, and it is not necessary for departures from the recommended practice to be disclosed in the financial statements. The first SORP, *Pension Scheme Accounts*, was published in May 1986.

In cases where there are matters of limited application, for example to a specific industry, these will be developed by the industry itself, and, if approved by the ASC, will become 'franked' SORPs. The first 'franked' SORP, entitled *Disclosures about Oil and Gas Exploration and Production Activities*, was issued in March 1986.

(c) A new form of consultative document, to be known as a 'Statement of Intent' (SOI) was to be introduced to enable the ASC to indicate at an early stage how it proposes to deal with a particular accounting matter. For example, the SORP, *Pension Scheme Accounts*, mentioned earlier, was preceded by an SOI published in November 1984.

The consultation process is a key feature of the development of standards, and is vital to ensure their acceptability by the profession and users of the financial statements. The full consultative sequence, of which the SOI is only one part, is set out below:

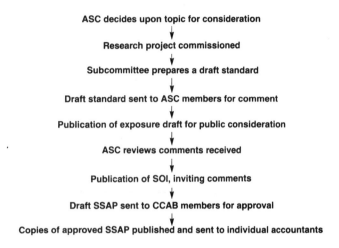

ASC decides upon topic for consideration
↓
Research project commissioned
↓
Subcommittee prepares a draft standard
↓
Draft standard sent to ASC members for comment
↓
Publication of exposure draft for public consideration
↓
ASC reviews comments received
↓
Publication of SOI, inviting comments
↓
Draft SSAP sent to CCAB members for approval
↓
Copies of approved SSAP published and sent to individual accountants

COMPLIANCE WITH STANDARDS

Members of the professional bodies which comprise the CCAB are expected to observe accounting standards in carrying out their responsibilities in connection with financial statements. This is not restricted to those qualified accountants who prepare the statements, but extends to members who are acting as auditors, and also members who act as company directors and are thus associated with their company's accounts, regardless of whether they had any part in their preparation. In cases where standards are not observed, significant departures should be disclosed unless this would be impracticable or misleading in the context of giving a true and fair view.

In cases of flagrant non-compliance with standards, the professional bodies have the sanction of bringing disciplinary action against the member concerned. Such actions are invariably well publicised and may result in the member being admonished, fined or, in extreme cases, excluded from membership.

STANDARDS AND THE COMPANIES ACTS

Whilst Statements of Standard Accounting Practice do not in themselves have legal status, the 1981 Companies Act (now consolidated into the 1985 Companies Act) included a number of points previously made in accounting standards. Several standards contain a note on legal requirements in Great Britain, indicating the degree to which the SSAP complies with relevant sections of the Act, and also gives guidance as to the treatment of items within the prescribed accounting formats.

STANDARDS AND THE COURTS

The first judicial recognition of standards came in the case of *Lloyd Cheyham & Co Ltd* v *Littlejohn & Co*. 1985. The plaintiffs alleged that they had lost money due to placing reliance on financial statements which, they claimed, had been audited in a negligent manner by the defendants. The auditors (successfully) defended their case by attempting to show that their audit was of a proper standard, and that the audited accounts complied with relevant SSAPs. In particular, the auditors' acceptance of the company's treatment of SSAP 2: *Accounting Policies*, SSAP 18: *Accounting for Contingencies* and SSAP 21: *Accounting for Leases and Hire Purchase Contracts* was called into question. The full details of the case are outside the scope of this book, but the case is important as, for the first time, the judge based his conclusions on the precise wording of the SSAPs. His judgement stated, *inter alia*, that accounting standards 'are very strong evidence as to what is the proper standard which should be adopted and, unless there is some justification, a departure from this will be regarded as constituting a breach of duty'.

UK STANDARDS AND INTERNATIONAL STANDARDS

In addition to the accounting standards produced by the UK profession, many other countries have their own 'national' standards. In 1973, an organisation, the International Accounting Standards Committee (IASC), was established with the object of harmonising standards on a world-wide basis. It has representatives from over seventy countries, and the members seek to encourage compliance between their own national standards and those agreed by the IASC. Many of the UK SSAPs have a section explaining the degree to which the standards accord with those issued by the IASC.

SUMMARY OF SSAPs
ISSUED TO DATE

SSAP	Title	Chapter
1	*Accounting for Associated Companies*	12
2	*Disclosure of Accounting Policies*	4
3	*Earnings per Share*	10
4	*Accounting Treatment of Government Grants*	5
5	*Accounting for Value Added Tax*	9
6	*Extraordinary Items and Prior Year Adjustments*	10
7	(withdrawn)	
8	*Treatment of Taxation under the Imputation System in the Accounts of Companies*	9
9	*Stocks and Work in Progress*	7
10	*Statements of Source and Application of Funds*	8
11	(withdrawn)	
12	*Accounting for Depreciation*	5
13	*Accounting for Research and Development*	6
14	*Group Accounts*	12
15	*Accounting for Deferred Tax*	9
16	*Current Cost Accounting**	Appendix
17	*Accounting for Post Balance Sheet Events*	11
18	*Accounting for Contingencies*	11
19	*Accounting for Investment Properties*	5
20	*Foreign Currency Translation*	13
21	*Accounting for Leases and Hire Purchase Contracts*	6
22	*Accounting for Goodwill*	6
23	*Accounting for Acquisitions and Mergers*	12

*The mandatory status of this statement was withdrawn on 6 June 1985.

A limited company's auditors must make reference in their report to any significant departures from standard accounting practice. The auditors' report (Fig. 3.1) refers to non-compliance with SSAP 19.

Figure 3.1 Laing Properties plc; non-compliance with SSAP 19

Laing Properties plc

AUDITORS' REPORT

To the Members

We have audited the financial statements on pages 12 to 27 in accordance with approved auditing standards.

As stated in the accounting policies, investment properties have not been included in the financial statements at open market value at 31 December 1985, contrary to the requirements of Statement of Standard Accounting Practice No 19.

As stated in the accounting policies, the presentation of reserves in the balance sheets as prescribed by the Companies Act 1985 has not been adhered to, for the reason stated. We do not concur with this departure from the requirements of the Act.

Subject to any adjustment which might be necessary as a result of valuing investment properties at open market value, in our opinion the financial statements, which have been prepared under the historical cost convention as modified by the revaluation of investment properties, give a true and fair view of the state of affairs of the company and the group at 31 December 1985 and of the profit and source and application of funds of the group for the year then ended and, except for the matter referred to in the immediately preceding paragraph, comply with the Companies Act 1985.

KMG Thomson McLintock

Chartered Accountants

London 18 March 1986

1   Discuss the aims and purposes of the Statements of Standard Accounting Practice and the duties of members of the accounting profession in relation thereto.

(15 marks)

(The Institute of Chartered Accountants in England & Wales, May 1986)

2

(a) What are the objectives of the Accounting Standards Committee and to what extent do you consider they are being achieved?

(12 marks)

(b) What are 'Statements of Recommended Practice' (SORP) and how may they be expected to influence financial reporting?

(8 marks)

(Chartered Association of Certified Accountants, Dec. 1984)

3   The managing director of a limited company has been told by the company's auditors that published financial statements should comply not only with relevant Acts of Parliament, but also with *statements of standard accounting practice* (SSAPs).

(a) Examples of areas covered by SSAPs include: 1. depreciation, 2. research and development expenditure and 3. stocks and work in progress.
Explain the reasons for standardising the accounting procedures in relation to *one* of these areas.

(8 marks)

(b) Explain the significance of SSAPs to the accounting profession and the users of accounting information.

(12 marks)

(University of London Schools Examining Board, June 1986)

E   Answers

1   Answers should make reference to the original objectives of the ASC (see answer to **2** below), and should stress the need for consistency and comparability. As regards the duties of members of the accounting profession, they are expected to observe SSAPs in carrying out their responsibilities in connection with financial statements. This applies equally to members who act as auditors or company directors, and are thus associated with the company's accounts, regardless of whether they participated in their preparation. Significant departures from the standards should be disclosed, unless this would be impracticable or misleading in the context of giving a true and fair view.

Mention should also be made of the disciplinary procedures which exist, *inter alia*, to take action against those members of the profession who, by their flagrant non-compliance with standards, bring the profession as a whole into disrepute.

2(a) The objectives of the ASC are: (1) to narrow the areas of difference and variety in accounting; (2) to recommend disclosure of accounting bases; (3) to require disclosure of departure from standards; (4) to introduce a system for wide consultation on standard setting; (5) to seek improvements in existing disclosure requirements of company law and the Stock Exchange.

The ASC has met its objectives to a considerable extent, although there is still work to do, particularly in respect of non-compliance by individual companies. The future role of the committee in relation to SSAPs is likely to be restricted to updating existing standards and introducing new standards only on matters of fundamental importance affecting the generality of companies.

2(b) SORPs were introduced as a result of a review of the standard-setting process which took place in 1983. They will cover matters which, whilst not being of fundamental importance affecting the generality of companies, still require authoritative pronouncements by the ASC to aid the development of accounting thought. The first SORP, *Pension Scheme Accounts*, was published in May 1986.

SORPs are not mandatory and there is therefore no need to disclose departures from them. Certain matters which are of limited application, for example to a specific industry, will be developed as SORPs by the industry itself and, if approved by the ASC, will become 'franked' SORPs.

It is expected that the influence on financial reporting will be similar to that of SSAPs.

3(a) (NB See Ch. 5, 6 and 7 for full details of the standards relating to depreciation, research and development and stocks and work in progress.)

Depreciation
There are many methods of depreciation used by companies and the standard lays down;

(i) the action to be taken if a change of method occurs;
(ii) the action to be taken on the revaluation of an asset;
(iii) that freehold land is not normally depreciated;
(iv) that increases in the value of assets should not stop depreciation being charged.

No one method of depreciation is laid down but the method chosen must be consistently applied.

Research and development
This divides research and development costs into:

(i) pure research;
(ii) applied research;
(iii) development expenditure;

and gives rules where expenditure may be written off in the accounting period in which it occurs and where it may be deferred to future accounting periods. Without this standard, companies might adopt a variety of treatments which would be misleading to the users of the financial statements.

Stocks and work in progress
This standard gives acceptable methods of valuation for stock and work in progress, including long-term contract work in progress (WIP). This is most important as the financial statements will be distorted if valuations are inaccurate. Disclosure must be made of the accounting policies adopted.

3(b) SSAPs represent an attempt by the accountancy profession to codify 'best practice'. Although not having legal standing, several standards have been incorporated in varying degrees within company law. The accountancy profession exerts considerable pressure on its members to comply with standards, and disciplinary procedures exist to deal with cases of flagrant non-compliance.

Users of accounting information expect, rightly, that the financial statements have been drawn up in the way recommended by the professional bodies. Failure to comply with SSAPs will probably result in statements which are misleading, inconsistent and useless for comparison with the accounts of other companies.

F A Step Further

The following references are given for the purpose of further study:
UK Statements of Standard Accounting Practice, Explanatory Foreword (ICAEW∗).
A Conceptual Framework for Financial Accounting and Reporting (ICAEW).

∗ The Institute of Chartered Accountants in England and Wales.

Chapter 4

Concepts, bases and policies

SSAP 2

A GETTING STARTED

The second SSAP, *Disclosure of Accounting Policies*, differs from all the other standards in that it addresses itself not to individual items appearing in the accounts or notes, but to the main concepts and assumptions on which the accounts are based. The standard is not an exhaustive list of concepts, and students should be aware that examination questions may require not only a knowledge of the concepts contained within SSAP 2, but also others such as 'materiality' and 'money measurement'. A summary of these is given later in the chapter.

B ESSENTIAL PRINCIPLES

SSAP 2: *DISCLOSURE OF ACCOUNTING POLICIES*

The intention of the standard is to establish ' . . . as standard accounting practice the disclosure in financial accounts of clear explanations of the accounting policies followed in so far as these are significant for the purpose of giving a true and fair view'. The following definition of *accounting policies* is given;

'Accounting policies are the specific accounting bases selected and consistently followed by a business enterprise as being, in the opinion of the management, appropriate to its circumstances and best suited to present fairly its results and financial position.'

Those accounting policies which are judged material or critical in determining profit or loss for the year and in stating the financial position should be disclosed by way of note to the accounts, with explanations being as clear, fair and as brief as possible. An example of one company's published accounting policies is given in Section C: Useful Applied Materials.

Before a company determines accounting policies which are relevant to its circumstances, it must have regard both to *fundamental accounting concepts* and *accounting bases*.

FUNDAMENTAL ACCOUNTING CONCEPTS

The standard is frank in admitting that its purpose is not to develop a basic theory of accounting, and as such does not include a comprehensive list of all accounting concepts. Instead, four fundamental concepts are referred to, which are the broad basic assumptions that underlie the financial accounts. They have '. . . such general acceptance that they call for no explanation in published accounts and their observance is presumed unless stated otherwise'.

If accounts are prepared on the basis of assumptions which differ in material respects from any of the generally accepted fundamental concepts, the facts should be explained. In the absence of a clear statement to the contrary, there is a presumption that the four fundamental concepts have been observed.

The four concepts are: going concern; accruals; consistency; prudence. The definitions contained within the standard are as given under the headings below.

The 'going concern' concept

The enterprise will continue in operational existence for the foreseeable future. This means in particular that the profit and loss (P&L) account and balance sheet assume no intention nor necessity to liquidate or curtail significantly the scale of operation.

The 'accruals' concept (also known as the 'matching' concept)

Revenue and costs are accrued (that is, recognised as they are earned or incurred, not as money is received or paid), matched with one another so far as their relationship can be established or justifiably assumed, and dealt with in the P&L account of the period to which they relate; provided that where the accruals concept is inconsistent with the 'prudence' concept (see below), the latter prevails. The accruals concept implies that the P&L account reflects changes in the amount of net assets that arise out of the transactions of the relevant period (other than distributions or subscriptions of capital and unrealised surpluses arising on revaluation of fixed assets). Revenue and profits dealt with in the profit and loss account are matched with associated costs and expenses by including in the same account the costs incurred in earning them (so far as these are material and identifiable).

The 'consistency' concept

There is consistency of accounting treatment of like items within each accounting period and from one period to the next.

The 'prudence' concept (also known as the concept of conservatism)

Revenue and profits are not anticipated, but are recognised by inclusion in the P&L account only when realised in the form either of cash or of other assets the ultimate cash realisation of which can be assessed with reasonable certainty; provision is made for all known liabilities (expenses and losses) whether the amount of these is known with certainty or is a best estimate in the light of the information available.

Problems in applying the concepts

The main difficulty in applying the four concepts is the fact that decisions have to be made as to the extent to which the expenditure of one year can reasonably be expected to produce revenue in future years, i.e. whether such expenditure should be carried forward on the balance sheet or written off to P&L account in the current year.

The standard refers to three specific areas of potential difficulty: the treatment of stocks and WIP, fixed asset valuation and research and development expenditure. Since SSAP 2 was issued in 1971, these matters have been covered in detail by various SSAPs, including SSAPs 9, 12 and 13, which are dealt with fully in later chapters of this book.

Accounting bases

Accounting policies, according to the definition given earlier, are specific accounting bases selected by the business as being best suited to a fair presentation of its results and financial position. The definition of 'accounting bases' is given as follows:

'The methods developed for applying fundamental accounting concepts to financial transactions and items, for the purpose of financial accounts, and in particular (a) for determining the accounting periods in which revenue and costs should be recognised in the profit and loss account and (b) for determining the amounts at which material items should be stated in the balance sheet.'

The standard gives a list of examples for which different accounting bases are recognised, several of which have become the subject of individual SSAPs including depreciation, deferred taxation, hire purchase and leasing and foreign currency conversion. As more SSAPs are published, the choice of accounting bases will diminish, but it is impossible to achieve a total and rigid uniformity, due to the complex nature of business activity.

Summary

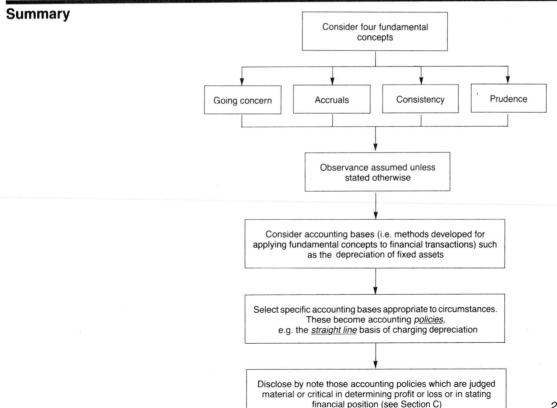

Consider four fundamental concepts

Going concern | Accruals | Consistency | Prudence

Observance assumed unless stated otherwise

Consider accounting bases (i.e. methods developed for applying fundamental concepts to financial transactions) such as the depreciation of fixed assets

Select specific accounting bases appropriate to circumstances. These become accounting *policies*, e.g. the *straight line* basis of charging depreciation

Disclose by note those accounting policies which are judged material or critical in determining profit or loss or in stating financial position (see Section C)

23

SSAP 2 AND THE 1985 COMPANIES ACT

The four accounting concepts stated in SSAP 2 are given statutory force within the 1985 Companies Act, which refers to them as 'fundamental principles'. In addition, the Act lays down two other principles, as follows:

1. It is not permissible to set off amounts representing assets or income against amounts representing liabilities or expenditure, or vice versa; and
2. In determining the aggregate amount of any item in the accounts, the amount of each component item must be determined separately.

The Companies Act also contains a provision which has a direct influence over the way in which the concepts are applied. Its effect is that the requirement to show a 'true and fair view' shall **override** the fundamental principles and all other requirements of the Act as to the matters to be included in a company's accounts or in notes to those accounts. In circumstances where a fundamental concept is abandoned, full details must be given in the accounts to comply with SSAP 2.

OTHER CONCEPTS

It has been stated earlier that SSAP 2 does not include a comprehensive list of accounting concepts. There follows a list of some of the more familiar ones which may be encountered in examinations.

The 'business entity' concept	The personal financial affairs of the owner or owners of the business should be kept separate from those of the business itself.
The 'cost' concept	The assets of the business should be recorded normally at the price paid for them, except where a diminution in value has occurred in which case the prudence concept requires that the lower value be incorporated. This concept is modified to the extent that it is usual for freehold land and buildings to be revalued, with the surplus (or, rarely, a deficit) being reflected in the accounts.
The 'duality' concept	The financial transactions of the business are capable of interpretation between value received and value given, and the basis of double-entry bookkeeping is that the sum total of the business's assets at any date will equal the sum total of the business's liabilities.
The 'money measurement' concept	It is assumed that the assets and liabilities of a company are capable of being measured in a common currency, regardless of the nature of those assets and liabilities. As an example, for a printing business, it becomes possible to add a stock of 100 000 sheets of paper to a collection of printing machines, by virtue of the ability to convert both types of asset into a common monetary form.
The 'materiality' concept	An item is likely to be material if knowledge of it might be expected to influence the user of the financial statements. The concept has practical application in that immaterial items require an accounting

treatment which is commensurate with their insignificance, or, to put it simply, an accounting mountain should not be made from a molehill!

The 'time intervals' concept	Financial statements are prepared for a period of time and events occur in either one period or another. These time intervals are essentially artificial accounting periods imposed upon the company for the sake of convenience and to enable comparisons to be made which are meaningful when one period is compared with another.
The concept of substance over form	Transactions and other events should be accounted for and presented in accordance with their substance and financial reality and not merely with their legal form. This concept is applicable in numerous areas of accounting, including that of consolidated accounts, whereby the legal existence of the individual group companies is ignored for the purpose of compiling group accounts, and also the practice, as per SSAP 21, of capitalising finance leases in a lessee's balance sheet, despite the fact that the lessee does not enjoy legal ownership of the asset which is being leased.
The objectivity concept	Financial statements should, as far as is possible, be presented in an unbiased manner and should reflect financial reality in a form which is as free as possible from the personal influences of either the owners of the business or the preparers of the statements.

C   USEFUL APPLIED MATERIALS

Companies are required to disclose the principal accounting policies which have been followed in preparation of the financial statements. Figure 4.1 is an extract from the annual report of a British television company.

Figure 4.1 TV-am Ltd; accounting policies

TV-am LIMITED AND SUBSIDIARIES

NOTES TO THE ACCOUNTS
For the year ended 31 January 1986

1 Accounting Policies

The principal accounting policies are

(a) Basis of accounting
The accounts have been prepared under the historical cost convention.

(b) Basis of consolidation
The group accounts consolidate the accounts of TV-am Limited and its trading subsidiary up to
31 January 1986.
In the company's accounts investments are stated at cost.
No profit and loss account is presented for TV-am Limited for the year ended 31 January 1986 as
provided by Section 228 of the Companies Act 1985. £4,706,000 of the consolidated profit
(1985 – £2,059,000 of the consolidated loss) for the financial year attributable to the shareholders
of the group has been dealt with in the accounts of the company.

(c) Tangible fixed assets
Tangible fixed assets are stated at cost.
Depreciation is provided at rates calculated to write off the cost less the estimated residual value
of each asset on a straight-line basis over its expected useful life as follows

Short leasehold interests	4% per annum
Mobile plant and technical equipment	25% per annum
Office furnishings and equipment	12½% per annum
Computer equipment	20% per annum
Technical installations	20% per annum

(d) Stocks
Stocks are stated at the lower of cost and net realisable value.

(e) Pension costs
It is the general policy of the company to fund pension liabilities, on the advice of external
actuaries, by payments to an insurance company. Payments made to the funds and charged in
the accounts comprise current and past service contributions. An independent actuarial valuation
on a going concern basis as at 1 April 1986 was carried out during May 1986, and showed the
scheme to be fully funded.
The scheme, which is contributory, is a defined benefit scheme. Membership of the scheme is a
condition of employment for all salaried employees, subject to age and qualifying period of
service requirements.

(f) Leases
The group has entered into operating and finance leases as described in Notes 10 and 19(b).
All lease rentals are charged to the profit and loss account in the period in which they arise.
Under the provisions of Statement of Standard Accounting Practice No.21, the group is not
required to capitalise its finance leases until the year ending 31 January 1989.

(g) Recognition of income
Income recognition is defined by transmission date.

1 Statement of Standard Accounting Practice No. 2 – *'Disclosure of Accounting Policies'* issued in November 1971, introduced important terminology, viz:
fundamental accounting concepts;
accounting bases;
accounting policies.

Required:
(a) Distinguish, briefly, between these three terms; (6 marks)
(b) State and explain briefly the fundamental accounting concepts.
(9 marks)
(Total 15 marks)
(The Institute of Cost and Management Accountants, May 1986)

2 The accounts of a medium sized public company have been prepared, but before they can be published certain notes must be drafted to explain the calculations of some of the figures in the accounts, and to show that the accounts conform to best accounting practice. As an accounting technician, you are a member of the team engaged in writing these notes, with special responsibility for the note on Accounting Policies.

Required:
(a) Name the four fundamental accounting concepts which under SSAP 2 are presumed to be observed when accounts are prepared, and indicate briefly what is meant by the terms 'Accounting Bases' and 'Accounting Policies'. Explain how the fundamental concepts are related to accounting bases and accounting policies. (13 marks)
(b) Give FOUR examples of matters for which different accounting bases may be recognised, including a brief explanation of how each one may have a material effect on the reported results and financial position of the business. (12 marks)
(Total 25 marks)
(The Association of Accounting Technicians, June 1983)

3 The word 'materiality' is used frequently in Company Law and in Statements of Standard Accounting Practice.
Required:
Briefly explain the concept of materiality, and state what criteria may be used to assess whether an item is material. (15 marks)
(Certified Diploma in Accounting and Finance, June 1985)

E ANSWERS

1(a) *Fundamental accounting concepts* are the broad basic assumptions which underlie the financial accounts, as recognised in SSAP 2.
Accounting bases are the methods developed for applying fundamental accounting concepts to financial transactions and items,

for the purpose of financial accounts.

Accounting policies are the specific accounting bases selected which are best suited to present fairly the company's results and financial position.

1(b) The four fundamental accounting concepts are as follows:

Going concern, which assumes that the business will continue in operational existence for the foreseeable future.

Accruals, whereby revenue and costs are accrued, i.e. recognised as they are earned or incurred, not as money is received or paid.

Consistency, whereby the accounting treatment of like items is applied consistently within each period and from one period to the next.

Prudence, whereby revenue and profits are not anticipated, but are recognised only when their realisation can be assessed with reasonable certainty. It also applies to the need for all known liabilities to be provided for, whether their amount is known with certainty or is a 'best estimate'.

2(a) See question **1 (a)**.

2(b) Four examples of matters for which different accounting bases may be recognised are:

Depreciation, as methods and rates used have a direct bearing on both the level of net profit and the net asset values.

Research and development expenditure, where the decision whether or not to capitalise development expenditure will affect profit levels and balance sheet totals.

Stocks and WIP, as different valuation methods will affect the levels of gross and net profit and balance sheet values.

Goodwill, where the decision as to whether it should be written off immediately, or carried forward over its useful economic life will affect the net profit level and balance sheet totals.

3 The concept of materiality is one of the most difficult to apply in a practical sense, as it depends upon subjective opinions of relative values. One definition of materiality states that an item is material if knowledge of it might be expected to influence the user of the financial statements. The purpose of classifying something as 'material' or 'immaterial' is that the accounting treatment of the item should be appropriate to its significance (or insignificance).

Criteria which may be used in determining whether an item is material are based on deciding upon the most appropriate yardstick for comparison. Although there is not at present a UK accounting standard on the topic, an attempt has been made by the *Australian* accountancy profession to give authoritative guidance on the subject. Paragraphs 16 and 17 of the *Australian* Accounting Standard No. 5 are reproduced below:

'16.   When considering the amount of an item, it should be compared with an appropriate base amount. The following base amounts should be used:

(a) Profit and loss statement items (including extraordinary items) should be compared with the operating profit for the current year or the average operating profit for the last five years (including the current year), whichever is the more relevant measure of profit having regard to the trend of the business over that period.

(b) Balance sheet items should be compared with the lower of:
    (i) total share capital and reserves, and
    (ii) the appropriate balance sheet class total, for example, current assets, non-current liabilities.

(c) Where an item is subject to comparison with the base amounts in both (a) and (b) above, the more stringent test should prevail.

'17 The comparison referred to in paragraph 16 should be guided by the following percentage limits:

(a) An amount which is equal to or greater than 10 per cent of the appropriate base amount, should be presumed to be material unless there is evidence to the contrary.

(b) An amount which is equal to or less than 5 per cent of the appropriate base amount should be presumed to be immaterial unless there is evidence to the contrary.

(c) The materiality of an amount which lies between 5 and 10 per cent of the appropriate base amount, is a matter of judgement depending upon the circumstances.'

F A STEP FURTHER

The following references are given for the purpose of further study:

G. A. Lee, *Modern Financial Accounting* (Van Nostrand Reinhold). Ch. 1.
J. Blake, *Accounting Standards* (Longman Professional Education Series). Ch. 3.

Chapter 5

Asset valuation (1): Government grants; depreciation; investment properties

SSAPs 4, 12 and 19

A   GETTING STARTED

Whilst most readers should be familiar with the various methods of charging depreciation they may be less certain about the reasons *why* it is charged. Two standards relate to the subject of fixed assets and their depreciation whilst a third looks at the problems involved when government grants are received, either towards the cost of fixed assets, or against revenue expenditure.

Questions are likely to:

1. Require a knowledge of the theory underlying depreciation;
2. Require a knowledge of the specific accounting treatments allowed by the standards;
3. Test the ability to compute depreciation, and record relevant details in the published accounts in accordance with Companies Act requirements.

B   ESSENTIAL PRINCIPLES

SSAP 4: THE ACCOUNTING TREATMENT OF GOVERNMENT GRANTS

Successive governments have provided assistance to business for various purposes, including the establishment of companies in areas of high unemployment and the provision of training schemes for young people. Such grants can be divided into those which relate to *revenue expenditure* (e.g. refunds of wages paid to trainees) and those relating to *capital expenditure* (e.g. financial assistance given towards purchasing machinery).

The accounting treatment is different for each type of grant, 'revenue-based' grants being credited against related expenditure in the same period, whilst 'capital-based' grants should be credited to profit and loss during the accounting period when related fixed assets are consumed. SSAP 4 permits two ways of doing this:

1. By reducing the cost of the fixed asset by the amount of the grant; or
2. By treating the amount of the grant as a 'deferred credit', a portion of which is transferred to revenue annually.

The arguments in favour of each method are:

First alternative: simplicity, as the reduced depreciation charge automatically credits the amount of the grant to revenue over the life of the asset.

Second alternative:

(a) assets acquired at different times and locations (i.e. some eligible, others ineligible) are recorded on a uniform basis, regardless of changes in government policy;

(b) control over the ordering, construction and maintenance of assets is based on the *gross* value;

(c) as capital allowances for tax purposes are normally calculated on the cost of an asset before deduction of a grant, adjustments to the depreciation charge shown in the P&L account are avoided when computing the amount of deferred taxation (see Ch. 9).

Note that two other possibilities were considered by the ASC; crediting the total grant immediately to P&L account, or crediting the grant to a non-distributable (i.e. not available for dividends) reserve. These were rejected on the grounds that the methods provided no correlation between the accounting treatment of the grant and the accounting treatment of the expenditure to which the grant relates.

The two acceptable treatments can be explained using an example of a machine costing £10 200 on which a grant of £1 800 is received. The machine is to be depreciated on the straight line basis over 3 years.

Method 1 Reducing the cost of the asset

Machine Account

Year 1 Cost	10 200	Year 1 Grant received	1 800

Depreciation Account

Year 1 Balance c/d	2 800	Year 1 P&L	2 800
		Year 2 Balance b/d	2 800
Year 2 Balance c/d	5 600	P&L	2 800
	5 600		5 600
		Year 3 Balance b/d	5 600
Year 3 Balance c/d	8 400	P&L	2 800
	8 400		8 400
		Year 4 Balance b/d	8 400

Profit and Loss Account

Year 1 Depreciation 2 800
Year 2 Depreciation 2 800
Year 3 Depreciation 2 800

Balance Sheet

Year 1 Cost 8 400 Less Depreciation 2 800   = 5 600
Year 2 Cost 8 400 Less Depreciation 5 600   = 2 800
Year 3 Cost 8 400 Less Depreciation 8 400   = NIL

Method 2 Crediting the grant to a deferred credit account	**Machine Account**			
	Year 1 Cost	10 200		

Divide over 3yrs.
1800
= 600 pa

Government Grant Account

Year 1 P&L	600	Year 1 Grant received	1 800
Balance c/d	1 200		
	1 800		1 800
Year 2 P&L	600	Year 2 Balance b/d	1 200
Balance c/d	600		
	1 200		1 200
Year 3 P&L	600	Year 3 Balance b/d	600

Depreciation Account

		Year 1 P&L	3 400	*10 200 ÷ 3*
		Year 2 P&L	3 400	
		Year 3 P&L	3 400	

Profit and Loss Account (year 1)

Debit		Credit	
Depreciation	3 400	Transfer from government grant a/c	600

(repeated for years 2 and 3)

Balance Sheet

Fixed assets
Year 1 Cost 10 200 Depreciation 3 400   = 6 800
Year 2 Cost 10 200 Depreciation 6 800   = 3 400
Year 3 Cost 10 200 Depreciation 10 200   = NIL
Accruals and deferred income*
Government grant

Year 1   1 200
Year 2   600

*A separate heading in the Companies Act balance sheet format. It is *not* part of shareholders' funds.

SUMMARY OF SSAP 4

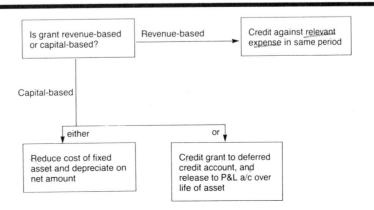

SSAP 12: *ACCOUNTING FOR DEPRECIATION*

SSAP 12 deals with the depreciation of fixed assets (defined as those assets which are intended for use on a continuing basis in the enterprise's activities) other than investment properties (see SSAP 19), goodwill (see SSAP 22), development costs (see SSAP 13) and investments, but including amounts capitalised in respect of finance leases (see SSAP 21).

Perhaps surprisingly, the standard makes, with one exception, no mention of the various *methods* of calculating depreciation, relying upon the management to 'select the method regarded as most appropriate to the type of asset and its use in the business so as to allocate as fairly as possible to the periods expected to benefit from the use of the asset'. The only reference to a specific method is where the standard states that 'although the straight line method is the simplest to apply, it may not be always the most appropriate.'

The standard concentrates instead on the circumstances in which depreciation should (or should not) be provided, and the way in which disclosure should be made in the financial statements.

The standard contains the following definition:

'Depreciation is the measure of the wearing out, consumption or other reduction in the useful economic life of a fixed asset whether arising from use, effluxion of time or obsolescence through technological or market changes.'

Depreciation should be allocated so as to charge a fair proportion of cost or valuation to each accounting period expected to benefit from the use of the asset. Note that depreciation is referred to as *amortisation* in the case of leasehold properties.

The amount to be allocated to accounting periods depends upon three factors.

1. The *carrying amount* of the asset (whether cost or valuation).
2. The *expected useful economic life*. Defined as the period over which the present owner will derive economic benefits from its use, it may be:

   (a) predetermined, as in leaseholds;
   (b) directly governed by extraction or consumption (e.g. quarries, mines);
   (c) dependent on its physical deterioration through use or effluxion of time;
   (d) reduced by economic or technological obsolescence. computers
   It is essential that asset lives are estimated on a realistic basis, and that identical asset lives are used for the calculation of depreciation both on a historical cost basis and on bases that reflect the effects of changing prices.

3   The *estimated residual value* at the end of its useful economic life in the business of the enterprise. The standard defines residual value as the realisable value of the asset at the end of its useful economic life, based on prices prevailing at the date of acquisition or revaluation, where this has taken place. Realisation costs should be deducted in arriving at the residual value.

CARRYING AMOUNTS

Although the term *carrying amount* is not specifically defined within the standard, it refers to the value placed on the fixed asset within the accounts for carrying over to the subsequent accounting period. This may be either the historical cost (which is the cost of acquisition or, in the case of self-constructed assets, the cost of production), or a revalued amount. The standard confirms that many companies revalue their fixed assets, in particular property, and states that the incorporation of revalued amounts gives useful and relevant information to the users of the accounts. The problems of depreciating revalued assets are dealt with later in the chapter.

REVISION OF ESTIMATES

Original estimates are revised occasionally in the light of technical and other considerations.

Revision of estimated useful economic life

This should be reviewed at least every 5 years, and more frequently where circumstances warrant it, with revisions to the estimates being made where necessary. If the enterprise has a policy of realistic estimation and regular review of asset lives, then there should be few fully depreciated assets still in economic use. Where future results would be materially distorted by this policy of regular review, the adjustment to accumulated depreciation should be recognised in the accounts for the period in which the revision is made, with the nature and amount of the adjustment being disclosed.

Revision of value

If at any time the net book value is considered to be irrecoverable in full (e.g. due to obsolescence or a fall in demand for a product) it should be written down immediately in the P&L account to the estimated recoverable amount, which should be charged to revenue over the remaining useful economic life. If the circumstances change so that an over-provision has been made, the provision can be written back to P&L account to the extent that it is no longer necessary. Note that the standard defines 'recoverable amount' as the greater of the net realisable value of an asset and, where appropriate, the amount recoverable from its further use.

Change in method of providing for depreciation

If a new method gives a fairer presentation of the results and of the financial position, then a change is permissible. In these circumstances, the unamortised cost should be written off over the remaining useful economic life by the new method, commencing with the period in which the change is made. Note that this does not represent a *change of accounting policy*, as the assets are being depreciated both before and after the date of the revision. Accordingly, no *prior year adjustment* (see SSAP 6) is required. Where an undepreciated asset owned for several years is to be depreciated for the first time, this not only represents a change of accounting policy, but also requires a prior year adjustment to be made, by charging the depreciation relating to prior years against the opening balance of retained profits.

REVALUATIONS

It is recognised that certain assets have a market value which is greater than net book value. In the year of revaluation, if account is taken of such increased value (by debiting the asset account and crediting an asset revaluation reserve account), an increased charge for depreciation will be required, based on the revised value. The standard requires that the *whole* of the depreciation charge should be reflected in the profit and loss account, and that no part of the charge should be set directly against reserves. This requirement was introduced into the 1986 revision of SSAP 12 in order to put a stop to the practice of distorting profits by 'splitting' the depreciation charge between that applicable to the historical value, which was charged in the usual way to P&L account, and that applicable to the excess of the revalued amount over the historical value, which was charged directly against the revaluation reserve.

If a company wishes to charge *supplementary depreciation* for the purpose of retaining profits for the subsequent replacement of fixed assets at prices higher than those upon which the depreciation charged in the P&L account has been based, it may do so by transferring profits from the appropriation account into a reserve specially designated for the purpose.

ASSETS NOT DEPRECIATED

Although *buildings* have a limited life and are therefore depreciated (other than 'investment properties'; see SSAP 19), the question of whether *land* is to be amortised is dependent upon whether it is freehold or leasehold, and whether it is subject to reduction in value by, for example, mineral extraction or changes in the desirability of its location. The following summarises the position:

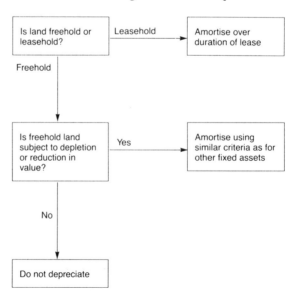

DISCLOSURE REQUIREMENTS

For each major class of depreciable asset, the following information should be disclosed:

(a) the depreciation methods used;
(b) the useful economic lives or the depreciation rates used;
(c) the total depreciation charged for the period;
(d) the gross amount of depreciable assets and the related accumulated depreciation.

The effect, if material, of any change in depreciation methods should be disclosed, together with the reason for the change. If assets have been revalued, the effect of the revaluation on the depreciation charge should, if material, be disclosed in the year of revaluation.

SSAP 19: *ACCOUNTING FOR INVESTMENT PROPERTIES*

Where a significant proportion of the fixed assets of an enterprise is held not for consumption in the business but as investments, the *current value* of such investments, and changes in that current value, are of prime importance for the proper appreciation of the financial position, rather than the *depreciated* value.

Investment properties are defined as: 'an interest in land and/or buildings:

(a) in respect of which construction work and development have been completed; and
(b) which is held for its investment potential, any rental income being negotiated at arm's length.'

The following are exceptions from the definition:

(a) A property which is owned and occupied by a company for its own purposes is not an investment property;
(b) A property let to and occupied by another group company is not an investment property for the purposes of its own accounts or the group accounts.'

The standard (which does *not* apply to charities) states that investment properties should *not* be depreciated but included in the balance sheet at their *open market value*. In the case of those held on short leases (i.e. 20 years or less) they should be depreciated in accordance with SSAP 12.

OPEN MARKET VALUE

↳ estimated net realisable value of the property

'Open market value' does not have to be determined by qualified or independent valuers, but the standard requires disclosure of the names or qualifications of the valuers, the bases used by them and whether the valuer is an employee or officer of the company. However, where investment properties represent a substantial proportion of the total assets of a major enterprise (e.g. a listed company) their valuation would normally be carried out:

(a) annually by a qualified person having recent experience of valuing similar properties; and
(b) at least every 5 years by an external valuer.

ACCOUNTING TREATMENT OF REVALUATIONS

Changes in the value of investment properties should not be taken to the profit and loss account, but should be disclosed as a movement on an *investment revaluation reserve*. If a deficit on revaluation exceeds the balance on the reserve then the difference shall be taken direct to the profit and loss account (an exception to this rule is made for investment trust companies and property unit trusts).

The balances of both the investment properties and the investment revaluation reserve should be displayed prominently in the financial statements.

C USEFUL APPLIED MATERIALS

Figures 5.1, 5.2 and 5.3 illustrate the relevant accounting policies adopted by three major UK public companies.

Figure 5.1 Tate and Lyle plc; policy re government grants

Grants

Investment and regional development grants are deducted from the cost of the relevant assets. Interest relief grants are deducted from net interest payable on a cash received basis.

Figure 5.2 Associated Dairies Group plc; policy re depreciation

(c) Depreciation

Depreciation is provided to write off the cost or valuation of tangible fixed assets, excluding freehold land, over their estimated useful lives, as follows:—

Freehold buildings and long leasehold property	67 years
Short leasehold property	over period of lease
Plant and equipment	3–20 years
Motor vehicles	4–10 years

(d) Government grants

deferred credit A/c ?

Method 2 Government grants in respect of expenditure on fixed assets are credited to a separate account and credit is taken in the profit and loss account over the estimated average life of the relevant assets.

Figure 5.3 Bryant Holdings plc; policy re investment properties

Tangible assets

Investment properties

On completion and substantial letting of commercial developments, interests in properties retained as investments are valued at their current market value and any surplus or deficit is dealt with through investment property revaluation reserve. Further valuations are made at annual intervals and the appropriate adjustments made. Depreciation is not charged on investment properties.

Method

1 Required:

(a) State possible alternative approaches to accounting for government grants which may be received by a company;

(5 marks)

(b) Discuss the reasons given for the rejection of certain of these approaches by the Statement of Standard Accounting Practice (SSAP 4) on this topic, and indicate what was recommended and why. (10 marks)

(Total 15 marks)

(Institute of Cost and Management Accountants, 1986)

2 SSAP 4 *The Accounting Treatment of Government Grants* permits a choice between two accounting methods for capital-based grants.

(a) What two methods are allowed? (7 marks)

(b) What are the main arguments in favour of each method?

(8 marks)

(15 marks)

(Chartered Association of Certified Accountants, Dec. 1983)

3 Most balance sheets include 'fixed assets at cost less depreciation' and an item which is usually significant in most profit and loss accounts is 'depreciation'.

Required:

(a) Define the term 'depreciation'; (3 marks)

(b) Explain why it appears in most profit and loss accounts;

(6 marks)

(c) Explain the purpose of showing fixed assets at 'cost less depreciation' in the balance sheet; (5 marks)

(d) Describe the usual methods of calculating the annual charge for depreciation for:

(i) published financial statement purposes, and

(ii) taxation purposes. (6 marks)

(20 marks)

(Certified Diploma in Accounting and Finance, June 1985)

4 You are required, in relation to Statement of Standard Accounting Practice No. 19 *Accounting for Investment Properties* (SSAP 19). to:

(a) define the term 'investment property';

(b) explain the accounting treatment of investment properties in the annual financial statements;

(c) state the arguments in favour of the treatment specified in SSAP 19. (10 marks)

(Institute of Cost and Management Accountants, Nov. 1985)

5 Toumey Enterprises plc owns three identical properties, North, South and East. North is used as the head office of Toumey Enterprises plc. South is let to, and is occupied by, a subsidiary. East is let to, and is occupied by, an associated company. A fourth property, West, is leased by Toumey Enterprises plc and the unexpired term on the lease is 15 years. West is let to, and is occupied by, a company outside the group.

Required:
(a) Which, if any, of these properties is likely to be an investment property of Toumey Enterprises plc and what additional information may be necessary for a final decision? State your reasons. (10 marks)
(b) Identify and justify the appropriate depreciation policy for each of the properties. (10 marks)
(20 marks)
(Chartered Association of Certified Accountants, June 1983)

E ANSWERS

1(a) Your answer should refer to the different treatment of grants which are revenue-based compared to those which are capital-based. There is only one possibility for the former (crediting against the related expenditure), but three alternatives were considered by the ASC for the latter:

(1) Crediting the grant to revenue over the useful life of the asset, by either:
(a) reducing the cost of the asset; or
(b) treating the grant as a deferred credit, being written back to revenue over the life of the asset;
(2) Crediting the entire grant to revenue on receipt; and
(3) Crediting the grant to a non-distributable reserve.

1(b) Alternatives (2) and (3) were rejected on the grounds that the methods provided no correlation between the accounting treatment of the grant and the accounting treatment of the expenditure to which the grant relates.

Alternative (1) was recommended, with either method being acceptable, for the reasons given in the answer to 2(b) below. The standard confirmed the treatment of revenue-based grants outlined in 1(a) above.

2(a) This answer will follow closely that given to 1(b) above, with the exception that a discussion of 'non-acceptable' methods is not required.
2(b) The argument in favour of reducing the fixed asset by the amount of the grant is *simplicity*, as the reduced depreciation charge automatically credits the amount of the grant to revenue over the asset's life. The alternative method (creating a deferred credit account) has the following advantages:

- uniformity of accounting treatment regardless of government policy;
- management control over assets is easier if based on *gross* values;
- adjustments are avoided in any deferred tax calculations.

3(a) Depreciation is the measure of the wearing out, consumption or other reduction in the useful economic life of a fixed asset whether arising from use, effluxion of time or obsolescence through technological or market changes.

3(b) Virtually all fixed assets have finite useful economic lives, and in order for the financial statements to reflect properly all the costs of the enterprise it is necessary for there to be a charge against income in respect of the use of such assets. This charge is referred to as depreciation.

3(c) By showing assets at 'cost less depreciation', the business is recognising the loss in value of the assets caused by use, effluxion of time or obsolescence.

3(d) The most common methods of calculating depreciation in the financial statements are the 'straight line' method and the 'reducing balance' method. For taxation purposes, 'writing down allowances' are calculated by using the 'reducing balance' method at rates determined by the government.

4 Parts (**a**) and (**b**) are explained within the chapter. Part (**c**) requires you to give the arguments in favour of the treatment specified in SSAP 19, and the following points can be stated:

(1) The current values of investment properties are held to be of greater importance than the depreciated values.
(2) Financial statements containing investment properties are more useful if the investments are shown at *current* values rather than at *historic* costs or valuations.
(3) Any depreciation which may occur will be automatically accounted for when assessing current values.

5(a)   The decision as to whether or not a property is classified as an 'investment property' must be taken by reference to the definition contained in SSAP 19, which states that an investment property is an interest in land and/or buildings:

(a) in respect of which construction work and development have been completed; and
(b) which is held for its investment potential, any rental income being negotiated at arm's length.

If property is owned and occupied by a company for its own purposes, or let to and occupied by another group company, then it does not come within the definition.

The four properties given in the question can be classified as follows:

North: not an investment property as it is owned and occupied by the company.

South: not an investment property as it is let to and occupied by another group company.

East: this is an investment property, as an 'associated company' is not a 'group company', according to the definition of a group contained in SSAP 14.

West: this is an investment property.

To confirm the above opinions on East and West, information would be needed as to whether the properties are held for their investment potential and the rental income has been negotiated at arm's length. In addition, all construction and development work must have been completed.

5(**b**) The acquisition or disposal of investment properties does not affect the manufacturing or trading processes of the business and consequently a systematic depreciation charge is considered irrelevant. It is the *current* value of such properties which is relevant to the users of financial statements. The only exception is a leasehold property with an unexpired term of 20 years or less. Such properties should be depreciated, to avoid the situation whereby a short lease is amortised against the investment revaluation reserve whilst the rentals are taken to P&L account. The appropriate policy for the four properties would be:

North and South: depreciate in accordance with SSAP 12.

East: not depreciated.

West: depreciate over 15 years.

F A STEP FURTHER

Many textbooks contain detailed appraisals of the SSAPs covered in this chapter, including:

J. Blake, *Accounting Standards* (Longman Professional Education Series).
Chs 5, 11 and Appendix.
R. K. Ashton, *UK Financial Accounting Standards* (Woodhead-Faulkner). Chs, 5 and 9.
Selected Accounting Standards – Interpretation Problems Explained (ICAEW), pp. 141–58.

Chapter 6	# Asset valuation (2): Research and development; hire purchase and leasing; goodwill

SSAPs 13, 21 and 22

A GETTING STARTED

In this chapter, we are looking at three standards which, despite covering very different areas, have the common thread of requiring decisions to be taken as to whether expenditure should be treated as capital or written off against revenue. In the case of goodwill, the question is asked whether it should be included in the financial statements at all.

Examination questions are likely to:

1. Test your knowledge of the permissible accounting treatments; and
2. Require an awareness of *why* particular accounting treatments are recommended.

B ESSENTIAL PRINCIPLES

SSAP 13: *ACCOUNTING FOR RESEARCH AND DEVELOPMENT*

Companies wishing to maintain or improve profitability often have to spend material amounts on researching or developing new or improved products, or new applications for existing products. Three categories of such expenditure are identified within the standard, as follows:

- *Pure* research, which is work directed primarily towards the advancement of knowledge.

- *Applied* research, which is work directed primarily towards exploiting pure research.
- *Development* expenditure, which is work directed towards the introduction or improvement of specific products or processes.

Such expenditure is often highly speculative in nature, with uncertainty being attached to the likely level of future revenues. Application of the *prudence* concept would result normally in it being written off against revenue in the year in which it is incurred. However, the standard recognises that, in certain closely defined circumstances, *development* expenditure may be deferred to be matched against future revenues (i.e. shown as a 'deferred asset' on the balance sheet), in accordance with the accruals concept.

DEFINITIONS

The standard, which does not apply to expenditure incurred in locating and extracting mineral deposits, contains the following definitions:

- **Pure (or basic) research**; original investigation undertaken in order to gain new scientific or technical knowledge and understanding. Basic research is not primarily directed towards any specific practical aim or application.
- **Applied research**; original investigation undertaken in order to gain new scientific or technical knowledge and directed towards a specific practical aim or objective.
- **Development**; the use of scientific or technical knowledge in order to produce new or substantially improved materials, devices, products, processes, systems or services prior to the commencement of commercial production.

NB The 'explanatory note' to the standard recognises that the dividing line between the three categories is often indistinct and particular expenditure may have the characteristics of more than one category.

ACCOUNTING TREATMENT

1. The cost of fixed assets acquired or constructed to provide R&D facilities is capitalised and written off over the useful life in the usual way (see SSAP 12).
2. All expenditure (other than on fixed assets) incurred on *pure and applied research* should be written off in the year of expenditure.
3. Development expenditure should be written off in the year of expenditure except in the following circumstances, when it may be deferred to future periods to the extent that its recovery can reasonably be assured:

   (a) there is a clearly defined project;
   (b) the related expenditure is separately identifiable;
   (c) the outcome of such a project has been assessed with reasonable certainty as to:
       (i) its technical feasibility; and
       (ii) its ultimate commercial viability considered in the light of factors such as likely market conditions (including

competing products), public opinion, consumer and environmental legislation;

(d) if further development costs are to be incurred on the same project the aggregate of such costs together with related production, selling and administration costs are reasonably expected to be more than covered by related future revenues; and

(e) adequate resources exist, or are reasonably expected to be available, to enable the project to be completed and to provide any consequential increases in working capital.

SSAP 13 requires all companies to choose between a deferral and write-off policy for development expenditure, and to apply this consistently. Note that the criteria for determining whether development expenditure may be deferred should also be applied consistently, and once a decision has been taken to write it off, it should not be reinstated as an asset, even though uncertainties which may have led to its being written off no longer apply.

The following mnemonic **DECORATION** may help you to remember the above criteria:

Defined project
Environmentally acceptable and commercially viable
Criteria to be applied consistently
Only defer as long as recovery can be assured
Revenues of future to more than cover further costs
Adequate resources exist for completion and working capital
Technically feasible
Identifiable expenditure
Once written off,
Not written back

AMORTISATION

If a decision is taken to defer development costs to future periods, their amortisation should commence with the commercial production of the product or process and should be allocated on a systematic basis to each accounting period, by reference either to the actual or expected sale or to use of the product or process.

A review of deferred development expenditure should take place at the end of each accounting period, and where the circumstances which originally justified the decision to defer no longer apply, or are considered doubtful, that proportion of the expenditure which is considered to be irrecoverable should be written off immediately.

DISCLOSURE IN ACCOUNTS

Deferred development expenditure should be separately disclosed, with movements in the period and the brought forward and carried forward balances being shown. The accounting policy followed should be clearly explained.

EXCEPTIONS

Apart from the exception relating to 'mineral deposits' mentioned earlier, the only other exception relates to companies which enter into firm contracts to carry out development work for third parties on such terms that the related expenditure is to be fully reimbursed, or to develop and manufacture at an agreed price which has been calculated to reimburse expenditure on development as well as manufacture. In such cases, any such expenditure not reimbursed at the balance sheet date should be included in *work in progress.*

SUMMARY OF SSAP 13

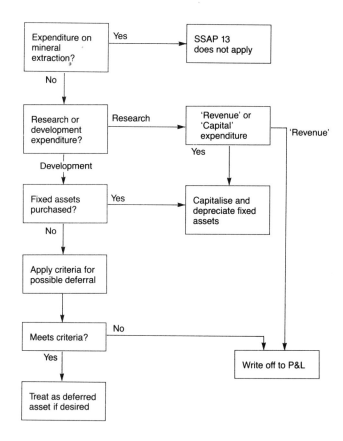

SSAP 21: *ACCOUNTING FOR LEASES AND HIRE PURCHASE CONTRACTS*

Leases and hire purchase contracts are means by which companies obtain the right to use or purchase assets. In the case of leasing, the ownership of the asset remains with the *lessor* (i.e. the original purchaser of the asset) and never passes to the *lessee* (i.e. the 'user' of the asset). With hire purchase contracts, however, the hirer of the asset may exercise an option to purchase the asset after certain conditions contained within the agreement have been met (e.g. the payment of an agreed number of instalments).

Until the implementation of this standard, companies which leased their equipment, vehicles, etc. did not show such items on their balance sheets, even though they may have accounted for a major part of the assets employed. Only the rental payments were disclosed in the P&L account. This treatment was felt to be misleading to users of the financial statements, and the standard now requires a company to include certain leased assets in its balance sheet, despite the fact that the company does not enjoy legal ownership of those assets.

The standard accounting practice is the same for both hire purchase and leasing contracts, and in the following text, the word 'lease' is used to describe both types of transaction.

OPERATING LEASE OR FINANCE LEASE?

The accounting treatment depends upon the classification of the leases between those which are 'operating leases' and those which are 'finance leases'. The explanatory note to the standard gives the following definitions:

An **operating lease** involves the lessee paying a rental for the hire of an asset for a period of time which is normally substantially less than its useful economic life. The lessor retains most of the risks and rewards of ownership of an asset in the case of an operating lease.

A **finance lease** usually involves payment by a lessee to a lessor of the full cost of the asset together with a return on the finance provided by the lessor. The lessee has substantially all the risks and rewards associated with the ownership of an asset, other than its legal title.

Note: In practice all leases transfer some of the risks and rewards of ownership to the lessee, and the distinction between a finance lease and an operating lease is essentially one of degree.

LESSEE'S BOOKS

The standard requires that a **finance lease** be capitalised (i.e. shown as a fixed asset under the subheading 'leased assets') in the lessee's accounts, despite the fact that the lessee is not the legal owner of the asset. This treatment recognises that, on occasions, the *substance* of a transaction should take precedence over its *legal form*, to ensure that the financial statements show as fair a picture as possible for the user. The explanatory note to the standard argues that it is not the asset itself, but the lessee's *rights in the asset* which are being capitalised. Note that, in addition to capitalising the asset, the obligation of the lessee to make future payments will be shown as a liability.

Rentals payable should be apportioned between the finance charge and a reduction of the outstanding obligation for future amounts payable. The finance charge is then apportioned to accounting periods so as to produce a constant periodic rate of charge on the remaining balance of the obligation for each accounting period (or a reasonable approximation thereof).

With an **operating lease**, the lessee need only show the rental as an expense in the P&L account, charged usually on a straight line basis over the lease term.

LESSOR'S BOOKS

The accounting treatment in the lessor's books is, in essence, the opposite of that applied to the lessee, with the amounts due from hiring out assets under **finance leases** being shown under 'debtors', the assets themselves being excluded from the fixed assets section of the balance sheet. Assets hired out under **operating leases** are capitalised, with rental income (excluding any service charges, e.g. for insurance and maintenance) being credited to P&L account.

Any initial direct costs incurred by a lessor in arranging a lease may be apportioned over the period of the lease on a systematic and rational basis.

Note that disclosure should be made of the accounting policies adopted for operating and finance leases in the financial statements of both the lessees and the lessors.

EXCEPTIONS

(a) A manufacturer or dealer lessor (i.e. where leasing is used as a means of marketing products, which may involve leasing a product to one customer or to several customers) should not recognise a selling profit under an operating lease. The selling profit under a finance lease should be restricted to the excess of the fair value of the asset over the manufacturer's or dealer's costs less any grants receivable by them towards the purchase, construction or use of the asset.

(b) Any profit or loss arising from a *sale and leaseback* transaction which results in a finance lease should be deferred and amortised in the financial statements of the seller/lessee over the shorter of the lease term and the useful life of the asset.

If the leaseback is an operating lease, any profit or loss should be recognised immediately, provided it is clear that the transaction is established at fair value. The standard contains provisions dealing with the situation where the price is above or below 'fair value'.

DEFINITIONS

Part two of the standard contains seventeen definitions of various terms relevant to hire purchase and leasing transactions. Some, including the basic definitions of operating and finance leases, have already been referred to, but the others are of some complexity and are outside the scope of this text. Reference should be made to Section G: A Step Further for useful guides to further study.

SUMMARY OF THE STANDARD

1. Accounting by lessees (main provisions only)

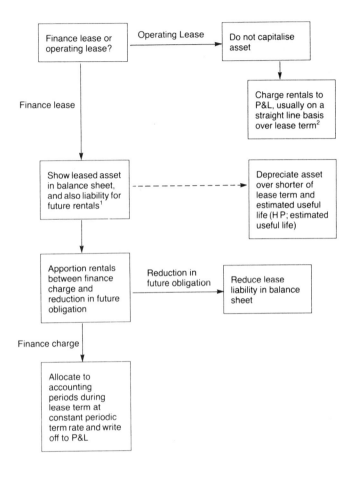

Notes:
1. To be divided between those payable in the next year, and amounts payable in the 2nd to 5th years inclusive from the balance sheet date.
2. Analysed between amounts payable in respect of hire of plant and machinery, and in respect of other operating leases.

2. Accounting by lessors
(main provisions only)

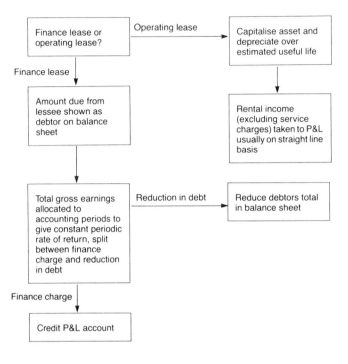

SSAP 22: *ACCOUNTING FOR GOODWILL*

Goodwill is the difference (positive or negative) between the value of a business as a whole and the aggregate of the fair values of its separable net assets.

- *Fair value* is the amount for which an asset (or liability) could be exchanged in an arm's length transaction.
- *Separable net assets* are those assets (or liabilities) which can be identified and sold (or discharged) separately without necessarily disposing of the business as a whole. They include identifiable intangibles (e.g. patents, trade marks, etc.).

If a goodwill figure has been calculated by using other than 'fair' values, it must be recalculated on a fair value basis, and if it includes material 'separable intangibles', these must be extracted and shown separately under an appropriate balance sheet heading.

Goodwill is incapable of realisation separately from the business as a whole, and has certain other characteristics which distinguish it from all other items in the accounts:

(a) the value of goodwill has no reliable or predictable relationship to any costs which may have been incurred;

(b) individual intangible factors which may contribute to goodwill cannot be valued;

(c) the value of goodwill may fluctuate widely according to internal and external circumstances over relatively short periods of time; and

(d) the assessment of the value of goodwill is highly subjective.

The standard makes an important contrast between **purchased** and **non-purchased** goodwill:

- **Purchased goodwill** is goodwill which is established as a result of the purchase of a business accounted for as an acquisition. Goodwill arising on consolidation is one form of purchased goodwill.
- **Non-purchased goodwill** is any goodwill other than purchased goodwill.

Non-purchased goodwill can arise whenever a going concern is worth more (positive goodwill) or less (negative goodwill) than the fair values of its separable net assets.

Whilst there is no difference in character between the two types of goodwill, *purchased* goodwill is established as a fact at a particular point in time *by a market transaction*. This is not true of non-purchased goodwill. *Because of this, it is not an accepted practice to recognise non-purchased goodwill in the financial statements.*

The standard expresses a preference for an immediate write-off of purchased goodwill (i.e. eliminating it against reserves in the year of purchase) on the grounds of consistency with the practice of not including non-purchased goodwill. It argues that if purchased goodwill is treated as an asset whilst non-purchased goodwill is not, a balance sheet does not present the total goodwill of a company; it reflects only the purchased goodwill of the acquired business at the date of acquisition, to the extent that it has not been written off.

The reasons given for writing off purchased goodwill against reserves rather than in the P&L account are:

(a) purchased goodwill is written off as a matter of accounting policy, that is, in order to achieve consistency of treatment with non-purchased goodwill, rather than because it has suffered a permanent diminution in value; and

(b) the write-off is not related to the results of the year in which the acquisition was made.

NEGATIVE GOODWILL

This arises when the fair value of the separable net assets acquired *exceeds* the fair value of the consideration given. It is the 'mirror image' of positive goodwill, and should be credited directly to reserves. Whenever negative goodwill arises, the fair values of the separable net assets will need to be reviewed particularly carefully to ensure that the fair values ascribed to them are not overstated.

ALTERNATIVE ACCOUNTING TREATMENT

Although the standard expresses a clear preference for the immediate write-off of purchased goodwill, it also allows companies to carry positive purchased goodwill as an asset, and to amortise it through the P&L account over the goodwill's useful economic life. In particular, it recognises that a company which makes an 'unusually large acquisition' may need to adopt the policy of amortising the goodwill, due to the effect which immediate write-off would have on its reserves.

An appendix to the standard gives guidance as to how the 'useful economic life' of purchased goodwill can be determined. It is defined as the period over which benefits may reasonably be expected to accrue from that goodwill which existed and was identified at the time of acquisition. Relevant factors include: expected changes in products, markets or technology; the expected period of future service of certain employees; and expected future demand, competition or other economic factors which may affect current advantages. Once the useful economic life has been determined, it cannot be subsequently lengthened, but it may be shortened.

If the purchased goodwill is to be amortised, it should not be revalued at a future date. A permanent diminution in value should be reflected by an immediate write down through the P&L account.

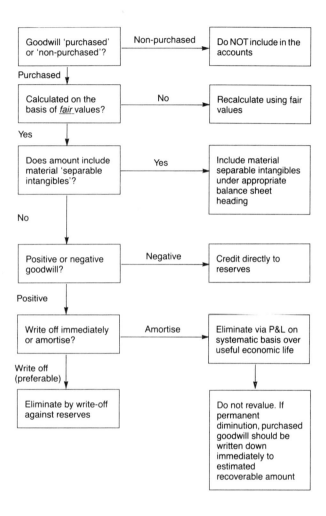

C USEFUL APPLIED MATERIALS

Figures 6.1, 6.2 and 6.3 illustrate the relevant accounting policies adopted by three UK companies.

Figure 6.1 DRG plc; Treatment of research and development expenditure

Research and development
Expenditure on research and development is written off in the year in which it is incurred except that the cost of laboratory buildings and plant is depreciated over the estimated useful lives of those assets.

Figure 6.2 Bardon Hill Group plc; Treatment of leased assets and assets on hire purchase

The net investment in leased assets and assets on hire purchase to customers is included in debtors. Finance charges are allocated to accounting periods over the lease period using the sum of the digits method.

The costs of both operating and finance leases are charged to the profit and loss account in the year in which they are incurred.

Figure 6.3 Guinness plc; Treatment of goodwill

Goodwill

Goodwill arises where the cost of acquiring new and additional interests in subsidiaries, related companies and businesses exceeds the net assets acquired and is written off directly to reserves.

The net assets of companies acquired are incorporated in the consolidated accounts at their fair values to the Group after making provisions for expected reorganisation costs including development losses. In addition, adjustments are made to reflect the alignment of accounting policies where the accounting policies of acquired companies would otherwise be inconsistent with those of the Group.

D RECENT EXAMINATION QUESTIONS

1

(a) Discuss the criteria which SSAP 13 *Accounting for Research and Development* states should be used when considering whether research and development expenditure should be written off in an accounting period or carried forward.   (10 marks)

(b) Discuss what extent these criteria are consistent with fundamental accounting concepts as defined in SSAP 2 *Disclosure of Accounting Policies*.   (10 marks)
             (20 marks)
(Chartered Association of Certified Accountants, June 1983)

2 Systemic Microcomputers plc are manufacturers of products which require a significant amount of 'research and development' expenditure. At the end of the company's financial year on 31 May 1986, an analysis of the general ledger account for 'research and development' expenditure showed the following:

	£
Cost of scientific apparatus	20 000
Cost of installing scientific apparatus	18 960
Salaries paid to staff engaged in pure research	31 200
Salaries paid to staff engaged on the development of a new product, codenamed 'Tudor'.........................	43 750
Salaries paid to staff engaged on the development of a new product, codenamed 'York'	28 120
	142 030
Less government grant received towards cost of scientific apparatus	4 000
	138 030

Notes

1. 'Tudor' is expected to become a viable and profitable addition to the existing product range.
2. 'York' has now been abandoned due to pressure from rival manufacturers.
3. A competitor, Macro Limited, is claiming £50 000 damages from the company for the alleged infringement of a patent which Macro Limited owns.
4. At a meeting held in April 1986, the company's directors authorised the purchase of laboratory equipment valued at £72 000. By 31 May 1986, contracts had been signed for two-thirds of this equipment.

Note: the company depreciates all tangible fixed assets over five years, with a full year's depreciation being charged in the year of purchase.

(a) Calculate the amounts to be included in the published profit and loss account and/or published balance sheet for each of the six items listed in the above analysis. Give reasons for the particular treatment adopted. (17 marks)

(b) The managing director of Systemic Microcomputers plc has asked for advice as to whether any reference to the matters contained in notes 3 and 4 above should be made in the financial statements for the year to 31 May 1986. Advise the managing director. (8 marks)

(University of London Schools Examination Board, June 1986)

3 In relation to SSAP 21 *Accounting for Leases and Hire Purchase Payments*:

(a) What is the difference between a finance lease and an operating lease? (10 marks)

(b) In preparing both the balance sheet and the profit and loss account of a finance company (the lessor) how should you treat:
  (i) an asset subject to a financial lease (6 marks)
  (ii) an asset subject to an operating lease? (4 marks)
  (20 marks)

(Chartered Association of Certified Accountants, Dec. 1985)

4 Nestor Ltd acquired Macaw Ltd in 1982 for a cost which resulted in the creation of goodwill amounting to £50 000 which has since been included in the consolidated balance sheet of Nestor Ltd as goodwill.

Requirement:
Advise the directors of Nestor Ltd on the various options available to them following the introduction of SSAP 22, *Accounting for Goodwill*, to deal with the goodwill in the accounts for the year ended 31 March 1986 and future years. (15 marks)
(The Institute of Chartered Accountants in England and Wales, May 1986)

E   ANSWERS

1(a) SSAP 13 draws a distinction between research expenditure and development expenditure. Research is divided between pure and applied, with pure research being defined as original investigation undertaken in order to gain new scientific or technical knowledge and understanding, but is not primarily directed towards any specific practical aim or application. Applied research is undertaken in order to gain new scientific knowledge and is directed towards a specific practical aim or objective. In both cases, research costs are written off in the year in which they are incurred, as they might not produce any benefits that extend beyond the current accounting year.

Development expenditure is the use of scientific or technical knowledge in order to produce new or substantially improved materials, devices, products, etc. prior to the commencement of commercial production. It may be deferred to future periods only if it meets the following criteria:

(a) there is a clearly defined project;
(b) the related expenditure is separately identifiable;
(c) the outcome of such a project has been assessed with reasonable certainty as to:
    (i)   its technical feasibility, and
    (ii) its ultimate commercial viability considered in the light of factors such as likely market conditions (including competing products), public opinion, consumer and environmental legislation and
(d) if further development costs are to be incurred on the same project the aggregate of such costs together with related production, selling and administration costs are reasonably expected to be more than covered by related future revenues and
(e) adequate resources exist, or are reasonably expected to be available, to enable the project to be completed and to provide any consequential increases in working capital.

1(b) SSAP 2 states four fundamental accounting concepts: (1) going concern; (2) accruals; (3) prudence; (4) consistency. The criteria listed in **1(a)** above are consistent with these four concepts to the following extent:

(i)   In item (d) of the listed criteria, there is a need to match expenditure with future revenues. This relates to the matching principle which is part of the accruals concept.

(ii) The prudence concept requires that revenue and profits should not be anticipated, and that costs should be written off as incurred unless the future realisation of revenue resulting from that expenditure can be reasonably expected, in which case the expenditure can be deferred. The concepts of matching and prudence may be in conflict, in which case prudence must prevail.

(iii) The going concern concept is relevant to item (e) in the listed criteria, which is concerned with the company having adequate resources available to complete the project. If there are doubts as to the company's status as a going concern, the development expenditure should not be deferred.

(iv) A consistent policy should be adopted to different projects in successive years.

2(a)

(1) £20 000 added to tangible fixed assets in balance sheet; £4 000 depreciation charged to P&L account – but see item 6 below. (Scientific apparatus is capital expenditure.)

(2) £18 960 added to tangible fixed assets in balance sheet; £3 792 depreciation charged to P&L account. (Cost of installation is treated as capital expenditure.)

(3) £31 200 shown as an expense in the P&L account. (Pure research is always written off.)

(4) Either £43 750 added to intangible fixed assets on the balance sheet, no depreciation until commercial production starts, or full amount written off to P&L account. (Development expenditure on viable products can be deferred to future periods, or written off as incurred.)

(5) £28 120 shown as an expense in the P&L account. (Expenditure on non-viable products to be written off.)

(6) Either deducted from the cost of scientific apparatus, with depreciation being adjusted accordingly, or shown as a separate fund on balance sheet, with £800 (1/5) being credited to P&L account each year for 5 years.

2(b)

Item 3: Claim to be noted as a contingent liability, with a statement of the maximum potential liability under the claim. A provision should be made in the P&L account unless there is a remote possibility of the contingency crystallising (see Ch. 11, SSAP 18).

Item 4: The Companies Act 1985 requires that capital commitments should be stated as a note to the financial statements. No accrual should be made in the P&L account.

3(a) An operating lease involves the lessee paying a rental for the hire of an asset for a period of time which is normally substantially less than its useful economic life. The lessor retains most of the risks and rewards of ownership of an asset in the case of an operating lease.

A finance lease usually involves payment by a lessee to a lessor of the full cost of the asset together with a return on the finance provided by the lessor. The lessee has substantially all the risks and rewards associated with the ownership of an asset, other than its legal title.

The nature of each lease will need to be determined from the terms of the contract between the lessor and lessee, as in practice all leases transfer some of the risks and rewards of ownership to the lessee, and the distinction between the two types of lease is essentially one of degree.

3(b)

(i) In preparing the financial statements of a finance company (the lessor), an asset subject to a finance lease would be recorded as follows:

The amount due from the lessee would be recorded as a debtor in the balance sheet. The amount will be the minimum lease payments, less the gross earnings allocated to future periods. The assets themselves are *not* recorded as fixed assets. The total gross earnings are split between those relating to the finance charge and those relating to the reduction in debt, with the former being credited to P&L account, and the latter reducing the outstanding balance shown as owing on the balance sheet.

(ii) An asset subject to an operating lease would be shown in the financial statements of a lessor as follows:

The asset should be recorded in the balance sheet as a fixed asset, and will be depreciated over its useful life in the normal way. The rental income from the lease will be credited to P&L account on a systematic and rational basis.

Disclosure should be made of the accounting policies adopted for both finance and operating leases in the accounts of the lessor.

4 SSAP 22, *Accounting for Goodwill*, draws a distinction between 'purchased' and 'non-purchased' goodwill, as follows:

- *Purchased goodwill* is goodwill which is established as a result of the purchase of a business accounted for as an acquisition. Goodwill arising on consolidation is one form of purchased goodwill.
- *Non-purchased goodwill* is any goodwill other than purchased goodwill.

From the facts given in the question, the goodwill in the consolidated balance sheet of Nestor Ltd is 'purchased goodwill'. The standard, in drawing the distinction between purchased and non-purchased goodwill, states that it is not an accepted practice to recognise non-purchased goodwill in the financial statements.

For purchased goodwill, the standard expresses a preference for an immediate write-off (i.e. eliminating it against reserves in the year of purchase) on the grounds of consistency with the practice of not including non-purchased goodwill. It argues that if purchased goodwill is treated as an asset whilst non-purchased goodwill is not, a balance sheet does not present the total goodwill of a company; it reflects only the purchased goodwill of the acquired business at the date of acquisition, to the extent that it has not been written off.

However, there is a possible alternative accounting treatment available, in that the standard allows companies to carry positive purchased goodwill as an asset, and to amortise it through P&L account over its useful economic life. This treatment recognises that a company which makes an 'unusually large acquisition' may need to adopt the policy of amortising goodwill due to the effect which immediate write-off would have on its reserves.

F A STEP FURTHER

The following references are given for the purpose of further study:
Accounting by Lessors (Deloitte, Haskins & Sells).
Accounting by Lessees (Deloitte, Haskins & Sells).
Guidance Notes on SSAP 21 (ICAEW).
Accountants Digest No. 178, SSAP 22: Accounting for Goodwill (ICAEW).
Selected Accounting Standards – Interpretation Problems Explained (ICAEW), pp. 1–26 (Research and development expenditure).

Chapter 7

Asset valuation (3): Stocks and work in progress

SSAP 9

A GETTING STARTED

'No area of accounting has produced wider differences in practice than the computation of the amount at which stocks and work in progress are stated in financial accounts.'

This preliminary paragraph to the standard (SSAP 9) underlines the importance of obtaining an accurate valuation of stocks and work in progress (WIP). Often a material amount in the business's balance sheet, over- or undervaluation results in distortions occurring in reported profit levels and net asset totals, whilst taxation may be under- or overpaid. In addition, an error in one year's stock figure has a 'knock-on' effect, in that the results of the succeeding year will also be distorted.

Limited companies must appoint a qualified *auditor*, whose job it is, *inter alia*, to report as to whether the company's accounts show a *true and fair view*. One of the major problems which auditors have is that of ensuring that the stock and WIP figures are reasonable. It is normal practice for them to attend the stock-taking to confirm that the physical quantities of stock and WIP have been correctly recorded, but this can, on occasions, be a highly specialised and even dangerous operation. (The author has unpleasant memories of scaling the outside of a 100-metre-high grain silo to perform part of a stock audit!)

Once the quantities have been audited, the next stage will be to confirm the valuations. The auditor will check them to ensure compliance with SSAP 9, and has the option of 'qualifying' his report on the accounts (i.e. drawing attention to matters with which he is unhappy) if he is dissatisfied with the way in which the valuations have been made.

SSAP 9: *STOCKS AND WORK IN PROGRESS*

Stocks and WIP comprise:

(a) goods or other assets purchased for resale;
(b) consumable stores;
(c) raw materials and components purchased for incorporation into products for sale;
(d) products and services in intermediate stages of completion; WIP
(e) finished goods.

The fundamental concept underlying the need to arrive at a stock valuation is the *matching* of cost and revenue in the *year in which the revenue arises* rather than the *year in which the cost is incurred*. If the revenue anticipated to arise (i.e. the net realisable value) is expected to be less than the cost incurred (e.g. due to obsolescence, deterioration or change in demand) then the irrecoverable cost should be written off to revenue in the year under review, in accordance with the prudence concept.

Thus, stocks and WIP normally are to be stated at **cost, or if lower, at net realisable value.**

Although we shall be considering in due course the detailed ways in which 'cost' is determined, it is useful at this stage to consider the following basic definitions:

Cost: '. . . that expenditure which has been incurred in the normal course of business in bringing the product or service to its present location and condition . . .'

Net realisable value: '. . . the estimated proceeds of sale less all further costs to completion and less all costs to be incurred in marketing, selling and distributing directly related to the items in question.'

The comparison of cost and net realisable value needs to be made in respect of each item of stock separately. Where this is impossible, groups or categories of stock items which are similar (referred to as 'fungible assets' by the Companies Act) will need to be taken together. If this were not the case, then material distortions could arise in the overall valuation as the following example shows:

Stock group	Cost (£)	Net realisable value (£)
A	50 000	90 000
B (damaged)	65 000	34 000
C	70 000	120 000
D (obsolete)	28 000	10 000
	213 000	254 000

If the 'lower of cost and net realisable value' rule were applied to the total stock, then this would give rise to a total of £213 000. However, this represents an overvaluation of £49 000 when we consider the results of applying the rule to the *individual* stock groups:

		£
A		50 000
B		34 000
C		70 000
D		10 000
		164 000

Failure to follow the rule would mean that the loss resulting from bad purchasing policies in respect of stock groups B and D, would not be written off, instead being carried forward to be set off against a prospective profit on items in stock groups A and C which has not yet been earned.

WHAT IS COST?

Although *net realisable value* is a relatively simple concept to grasp, the *cost* of stock is rather more complicated. The price paid for the asset *might* be easily ascertained, e.g. from a purchase invoice. However, in many cases, the price paid cannot be matched to actual goods, due, perhaps, to the physical nature of the stock. For example, petrol might be delivered to a garage on fifty separate occasions and at fifty separate prices during an accounting year. The stock of petrol at the end of the year may be 'cheap' petrol, 'expensive' petrol, or, more likely, a mixture of prices. No amount of expertise could determine this, and so *theoretical* pricing models have been created for this purpose (e.g. FIFO, AVCO, etc.) which are looked at later in the chapter.

A point made in *International* Accounting Standard 2 is that, even if the price paid can be identified with specific goods held in stock, some form of theoretical pricing model is still desirable, since otherwise management might manipulate profit by choosing which batch of stock should be sold.

The principle to be adopted is that the methods used in allocating costs to stocks and WIP need to be selected with a view to providing the *fairest possible approximation to the expenditure actually incurred in bringing the product to its present location and condition.*

The explanatory note to the standard gives, as an example, the case of retail stores holding a large number of rapidly changing individual items, where stocks on the shelves have often been stated at current selling prices less the normal gross profit margin. In *these particular circumstances* this may be acceptable as being the only practical method of arriving at a figure which approximates to cost.

In addition to the problem of determining the price paid for the stock, there is the added complication of determining any other relevant 'expenditure actually incurred in bringing the product to its present location and condition'. Thus SSAP 9 opts for an *absorption* costing approach in the financial accounts. This is in stark contrast to the view of most authorities on management accounting, who advocate *marginal* costing as more appropriate for management decision-making.

The standard recognises that the majority of problems arising in practice in determining both the cost and the net realisable value result from considerations which are relevant to *particular* businesses, and are 'not of such universal application that they can be the subject of a statement of standard accounting practice'. Because of this, an Appendix (Appendix 1) to the standard sets out general guidelines as to the particular areas of difficulty (see 'Practical difficulties' below).

To put these difficulties into context, the *full* definitions of key phrases used by the standard in connection with stocks and WIP are given under the heading below:

DEFINITIONS

Cost is defined in relation to the different categories of stocks and WIP as being that expenditure which has been incurred in the normal course of business in bringing the product or service to its present location and condition. This expenditure should include, in addition to *cost of purchase*, such *costs of conversion* as are appropriate to that location or condition.

Cost of purchase comprises purchase price including import duties, transport and handling costs and any other directly attributable costs, less trade discounts, rebates and subsidies.

Cost of conversion comprises:

(a) costs which are specifically attributable to units of production, i.e. direct labour, direct expenses and subcontracted work;

(b) production overheads;

(c) other overheads, if any, attributable in the particular circumstances of the business to bringing the product or service to its present location and condition.

Production overheads: overheads incurred in respect of materials, labour or services for production, based on the normal level of activity, taking one year with another. For this purpose each overhead should be classified according to function (e.g. production, selling or administration) so as to ensure the inclusion in cost of conversion of those overheads (including depreciation) which relate to production, notwithstanding that these may accrue wholly or partly on a time basis.

Net realisable value: the actual selling or estimated selling price (net of trade but before settlement discounts) less:

(a) all further costs to completion; and

(b) all costs to be incurred in marketing, selling and distributing.

PRACTICAL DIFFICULTIES

1. The allocation of overheads

The allocation of overheads included in the valuation of stocks and WIP needs to be based on the company's *normal* level of activity taking one year with another. 'Normality' is determined by reference to such factors as:

1. The volume of production which the production facilities are intended by their designers and by management to produce under prevailing working conditions; and
2. The budgeted and actual levels of activity for the year under review and the ensuing year.

The definition of cost given earlier includes the words 'incurred in the normal course of business' when referring to the circumstances in which expenditure can be included in the valuation. The corollary of this is that all *abnormal* conversion costs need to be excluded.

The costing methods adopted by a business are usually designed to ensure that all *direct* costs (materials, labour and direct expenses) are identified and charged on a reasonable and consistent basis. Problems arise regarding certain overheads which require the exercise of subjective judgement as to their allocation.

Specific costs referred to in Appendix 1 of the standard are as follows:

Cost	Include in stock valuation?
• Exceptional spoilage	No (abnormal)
• Idle capacity	No (abnormal)
• Design, marketing and selling costs incurred before manufacture	Yes (if firm sales contract)
• Costs of general management (larger organisations)	No (not directly related to production)
• Costs of general management (small organisation where management involved in daily administration of the various functions)	Yes (if part of cost can be allocated to production function)
• Central service departments	Yes (but only those costs related to production function)
• Marginal costs in management accounts	Yes (but add appropriate proportion of those production overheads not already included in the marginal cost)

2. Methods of costing

The difficulties of relating prices to stock items have been mentioned earlier, and Appendix 1 to the Standard, whilst not explicitly favouring any one valuation method, does require management to:

'exercise judgement to ensure that the methods chosen provide the fairest practicable approximation to actual cost'.

Appendix 2 to the standard contains a glossary of terms which includes seven stock valuation methods. The following is a summary of them, together with a comment regarding their 'acceptability' for the purposes of SSAP 9.

Method	Acceptable?
Unit cost	
• The cost of purchasing or manufacturing identifiable units of stock	Yes
Average cost	
• Using an average price computed by dividing the total cost of units by the total number of such units	Yes
FIFO (first in first out)	
• Using the assumption that the stock on hand represents the latest purchases or production	Yes
LIFO (last in first out)	
• Using the assumption that the stock on hand represents the earliest purchases or production	No, as costs are unlikely to bear a reasonable relationship to actual costs obtaining during the period
Base stock	
• Ascribing a fixed unit value to a predetermined number of units in stock, any excess over this number being valued on the basis of some other method	No, for the same reasons as given for LIFO
Replacement cost	
• The cost at which an identical asset could be purchased or manufactured	No, except in certain circumstances, e.g. where the value of the raw material content is a high proportion of the total stock value, and the raw material price fluctuates considerably
Standard cost	
• Using predetermined costs calculated from management's estimates of expected levels of costs	Yes, provided that the standard costs are reviewed frequently to ensure that they bear a reasonable relationship to actual costs

In addition, two other methods are referred to in Appendix 1 of the standard:

Selling price less estimated profit margin
- Sales prices of stock on hand, less the expected gross profit percentage

No, unless it can be demonstrated that it gives a reasonable approximation of actual cost

Latest purchase price
- Applying latest purchase price to the total units in stock

No, as it is not necessarily the same as actual costs and, in times of rising prices will result in the taking of a profit which has not been realised

LONG-TERM CONTRACT WORK IN PROGRESS

Special consideration is given in the standard to the valuation of long-term contract WIP. This is defined as:

A contract entered into for manufacture or building of a single substantial entity or the provision of a service where the time taken to manufacture, build or provide is such that a substantial proportion of all such contract work will extend for a period exceeding one year.

Due to the length of time taken for such contracts, it is felt to be reasonable to take credit for a proportion of profit arising whilst the contracts are in progress.

The profit, if any, should reflect the proportion of the work carried out at the accounting date. If the outcome of the contract is uncertain, then it may be prudent not to take up any profit. If, however, a *loss* is expected, then a provision needs to be made for the whole of the loss as soon as it is recognised. Any 'progress payments' (i.e. payments made by a customer at intervals during the contract) received or receivable are deducted from the total of costs incurred, when calculating the profit or loss.

The accounting treatment of long-term contract WIP can be summarised therefore as follows:

The gross amount of long-term contract WIP should be stated at cost plus attributable profit (if any) less foreseeable losses (if any).

The standard gives the following definitions of *attributable profit* and *foreseeable losses*:

Attributable profit: that part of the total profit currently estimated to arise over the duration of the contract (after allowing for likely increases in costs so far as not recoverable under the terms of the contract) which fairly reflects the profit attributable to that part of the work performed at the accounting date. (There can be no attributable profit until the outcome of the contract can be assessed with reasonable certainty.)

Foreseeable losses: losses which are currently estimated to arise over the duration of the contract (after allowing for estimated remedial and maintenance costs, and increases in costs so far as not recoverable under the terms of the contract). This estimate is required irrespective of;

(a) whether or not the work has yet commenced on such contracts;
(b) the proportion of work carried out at the accounting date;
(c) the amount of profits expected to arise on other contracts.

As a further acknowledgement of the need for 'prudence', and to provide against contingencies, many businesses apply a fractional reduction to the profit calculation, with a typical formula being:

$$2/3 \times \left\{ (\text{Total contract price} - \text{Total costs [actual and estimated]}) \times \frac{\text{Work certified}}{\text{Total contract price}} \right\}$$

SSAP 9 v. SSAP 2

The standard requires the calculation of attributable profits to be made on a *prudent* basis, and only when the outcome can be reasonably foreseen. It also requires losses to be recognised immediately. In these respects, SSAP 9 does follow the prudence concept. However, some would argue that the recognition of *any* profit prior to the completion of a contract is imprudent, and in conflict with the 'accruals' concept. It is worth remembering at this point that SSAP 2 states that 'where the accruals concept is inconsistent with the "prudence" concept, the latter prevails'.

DISCLOSURE IN FINANCIAL STATEMENTS

Relevant extracts from accounts of public companies are given in Section C. Useful Applied Materials. The standard requires:

- accounting policies to be stated;
- stocks and WIP to be subclassified in the balance sheet or in notes 'in a manner which is appropriate to the business';
- in relation to long-term WIP, there should be stated:
  (a) the amount of WIP at cost plus attributable profit, less foreseeable losses;
  (b) cash received and receivable at the accounting date as progress payments on account of contracts in progress.

C USEFUL APPLIED MATERIALS

Figures 7.1, 7.2 and 7.3 are taken from the annual reports of major UK public companies.

Figure 7.1 Associated British Foods plc; valuation of stocks

Stocks

Stocks are generally valued at the lower of cost and net realisable value, after making due provision against obsolete and slow-moving items. In the case of finished goods the term 'cost' includes ingredients, production wages and production overheads.

Figure 7.2 Tate and Lyle plc; valuation of stocks and contract work in progress

Valuations of stocks and contract work in progress

Stocks, other than those stocks of sugar and molasses to which reference is made under 'Trading in commodities', are valued at direct cost plus attributable overheads, or net realisable value if lower. Long term contract work in progress is shown at cost plus attributable profits less foreseeable losses and progress payments received and receivable.

Figure 7.3 Tarmac plc; valuation of stocks and long-term contract work in progress

Stocks	Stocks are valued at the lower of cost and net realisable value. Cost includes appropriate overheads.
Long term contract work in progress	Long term contract work in progress is valued at cost plus attributable profit less any foreseeable losses. Payments received on account are deducted in arriving at the group balance sheet figure.

D RECENT EXAMINATION QUESTIONS

1

(a) 'Both cost and net realisable value must be calculated for the stocks and work in progress at the balance sheet date and whichever of these gives the lower figure will appear in the accounts.'
Critically evaluate this statement.

(13 marks)

(b) Motac Enterprises commenced the manufacture of lockable petrol tank caps on 1 July 1984. By 31 December 1984 when the half yearly financial reports were prepared, 2 000 complete petrol caps and 200 half-finished (as regards materials, labour and factory overheads) petrol caps were produced. No orders from customers had yet been taken. Costs in the six-month period were as follows:

	£
Materials consumed	1 650
Labour	2 160
Production overheads	390
Administrative overheads	270
	4 470

At 31 December 1984 it was estimated that the net realisable value of each completed petrol cap was £2.75. At this date, the firm held stocks of raw materials as follows:

	Cost (£)	Net realisable value (£)
Material X	1 200	1 370
Material Y	300	240
Material Z	530	680

Required:
Acceptable valuations for:
(i)   raw materials;
(ii) work in progress: and
(iii) finished goods at 31 December 1984.   (12 marks)
(Total 25 marks)
(Institute of Chartered Secretaries and Administrators June 1985)

2   Explain the meaning and significance of the following terms as they relate to the valuation of stocks and work in progress:

(i)   'Cost of purchase' and 'Cost of conversion'.   (Subtotal 5 marks)
(ii) 'Net realisable value' and 'Replacement cost'.
                                                     (Subtotal 5 marks)
(iii) 'Long-term contract'.   (Subtotal 4 marks)
(iv) 'Attributable profit' and 'Foreseeable losses'.
                                                     (Subtotal 4 marks)
                                                     (Total 18 marks)
                                          (LCCI Higher Stage,1984)

3   Fox Ltd is a construction company which undertakes long-term contracts. On 13 July 1984 it commenced a contract to build an office block for an agreed fixed price of £750 000. The forecast completion date is 31 March 1986. Fox Ltd makes up its accounts to 30 September. The following financial information is provided for the contract:

30 September	1984 (£)	1985 (£)
Costs to date	50 000	500 000
Estimated costs to completion	550 000	125 000
Value of work certified as complete	25 000	600 000
Progress payments received	20 000	425 000

Required:
(a) Prepare balance sheet valuations of the contract at 30 September 1984 and 30 September 1985, in accordance with the instructions contained in Statement of Standard Accounting Practice 9 entitled 'Stocks and Work in Progress' with an explanation of the procedures you adopt.   (10 marks)
(b) Compare and contrast the procedures for valuing long-term work in progress with the conventional method for valuing stock

and work in progress. Explain fully the reasons for the different approaches.   (12 marks)

(Total 22 marks)

(Institute of Chartered Secretaries and Administrators, Dec. 1985)

E ANSWERS

1(a) SSAP 9 states that stocks and WIP should normally be stated at cost, or if lower, at net realisable value. Definitions contained within the standard are:

Cost: that expenditure which has been incurred in the normal course of business in bringing the product or service to its present location or condition. This expenditure should include, in addition to cost of purchase, such costs of conversion as are appropriate to that location or condition.

(Cost of purchase, cost of conversion and net realisable value are defined in the answer to question **2** below.)

Various valuation methods have been devised to overcome the difficulties of relating prices of stock items, including LIFO, FIFO and average cost. Whilst the standard does not explicitly favour any one method, it does require management to exercise judgement to ensure that the methods chosen provide the fairest practicable approximation to actual cost.

1(b) *Raw materials*: lower of cost and net realisable value for each separate item of stock:

Material X £1 200
Material Y £   240
Material Z £   530

£1 970

Work in progress (200 half-completed petrol caps): £4 470 was the total cost for 2 000 complete and 200 half-complete petrol caps. Excluding the administrative overheads, the cost per 'equivalent unit' is £4 200 ÷ 2 100 = £2, which is lower than the net realisable value. The valuation of the WIP is therefore 200 × (½ × £2) = £200.

Finished goods: value 2 000 × £2 = £4 000.

2(i) Cost of purchase comprises purchase price including import duties, transport and handling costs and any other directly attributable costs, less trade discounts, rebates and subsidies.

Cost of conversion comprises:

(a) costs which are specifically attributable to units of production, i.e. direct labour, direct expenses and subcontracted work;

(b) production overheads;

(c) other overheads, if any, attributable in the particular circumstances of the business to bringing the product or service to its present location and condition.

When determining the valuation of stocks and WIP, cost price should include, in addition to cost of purchase, such costs of conversion as are appropriate.

2(ii) Net realisable value is the actual selling or estimated selling price (net of trade but before settlement discounts) less:

(a) all further costs to completion; and

(b) all costs to be incurred in marketing, selling and distributing.

Replacement cost is the cost at which an identical asset could be purchased or manufactured.

SSAP 9 requires that stocks and WIP be stated at the lower of cost and net realisable value. However, in certain circumstances replacement cost can be used for valuation purposes, e.g. where the value of raw material content is a high proportion of the total stock value, and the raw material price fluctuates considerably.

2(iii) A long-term contract is a contract entered into for manufacture or building of a single substantial entity or the provision of a service where the time taken to manufacture, build or provide is such that a substantial proportion of all such contract work will extend for a period exceeding one year.

SSAP 9 recognises that it is reasonable to take credit for a proportion of the profit arising on long-term contract WIP, provided that the calculation is made on a prudent basis.

2(iv) *Attributable profit*: that part of the total profit currently estimated to arise over the duration of the contract (after allowing for likely increases in costs so far as not recoverable under the terms of the contract) which fairly reflects the profit attributable to that part of the work performed at the accounting date. (There can be no attributable profit until the outcome of the contract can be assessed with reasonable certainty.)

Foreseeable losses: losses which are currently estimated to arise over the duration of the contract (after allowing for estimated remedial and maintenance costs, and increases in costs so far as not recoverable under the terms of the contract). This estimate is required irrespective of:

(a) whether or not the work has yet commenced on such contracts;

(b) the proportion of work carried out at the accounting date;

(c) the amount of profits expected to arise on other contracts.

The accounting treatment of long-term contract WIP is that it should be stated at cost plus attributable profits (if any) less foreseeable losses (if any).

3(a) As the contract had only recently commenced at 30 September 1984, it is not appropriate under these circumstances to assess any attributable profit. It should be valued at cost incurred to date, £50 000, less progress payments received, £20 000 = £30 000.

At 30 September 1985, however, the contract is well under way and the outcome can be assessed with reasonable certainty. Although SSAP 9 does not require a fractional reduction to be made for the sake of prudence when assessing contract valuation, it is conventional practice to do so, with the calculation of attributable profit being:

$$2/3 \times \left\{ (\pounds750\ 000 - \pounds625\ 000) \times \frac{\pounds600\ 000}{\pounds750\ 000} \right\} = \pounds66\ 667$$

The WIP valuation is then; $(500{,}000 - 425{,}000) + 66\ 667 = \pounds141\ 667$

3(b) The conventional method for valuing stocks and WIP is on the basis of the lower of cost and net realisable value, with no profit element being incorporated in the valuation. With the valuation of long-term contract WIP, however, it is felt to be reasonable to take credit for a proportion of profit arising whilst the contracts are in progress.

If the outcome of the contract is uncertain, then it may be prudent not to take up any profit. If a loss is expected, then a provision needs to be made for the whole of the loss as soon as it is recognised.

F A STEP FURTHER

The following references are given for the purpose of further study:

F. A. J. Couldery, *Accounting Standards Study Book* (Gee). Ch. 9.
J. Blake, *Accounting Standards* (Longman Professional). Ch. 9.
J. H. F. Gemmell, *How to Value Stock; a guide to industry practices* (ICAEW).
Selected Accounting Standards – Interpretation Problems Explained (ICAEW), pp. 301–26.

Chapter 8

Funds flow analysis: Statements of source and application of funds

SSAP 10

A   GETTING STARTED

Many students who are endowed with a knowledge of accountancy principles and practices may be forgiven for thinking that the production of financial statements is an end in itself, and that accounting information is written in a code which can only (and *should* only) be 'cracked' by other accountants. However, this is not an accurate portrayal, since accountancy should be seen to be a *means to an end*, whereby financial information is *accessible* not only to those with an understanding of accounting, but also to those without such an advantage.

'Accessibility' can be achieved in a number of ways, including:

- Clear presentation of reports.
- Use of graphics and photographs as an aid to clarity in the annual report.
- The production of 'employee reports', which are condensed and simplified versions of the full annual report, often presented in a visually attractive style.
- The provision of shareholder information services by companies to allow individual shareholders to query or comment upon the company's performance.
- Encouragement and incentives given to shareholders to attend their company's Annual General Meeting (e.g. a confectionery company might offer a pack of 'free samples' to each shareholder in attendance).

- The inclusion of a statement of source and application of funds within the annual report, to explain, in layman's language, the ways by which the company derived its funds during the year, and the uses made of them.

The importance of the last mentioned item, the Statement of Source and Application of Funds (SSAF), has been recognised by the requirement in SSAP 10 that all enterprises with an annual turnover in excess of £25 000 shall include such a statement within their audited annual accounts.

Questions on this topic tend to concentrate on the mechanics of preparation of the statement rather than on the precise content of the standard, but the SSAP gives useful guidance as to the favoured ways of presenting the information.

B ESSENTIAL PRINCIPLES

SSAP 10: *STATEMENTS OF SOURCE AND APPLICATION OF FUNDS*

Whilst a P&L account shows the revenue position of the business during the financial year, and the balance sheet shows the capital position at the end of the year (with comparative figures giving the opening position), it is also desirable to identify the movements in assets, liabilities and capital which have taken place during the year and the resultant effect on *net liquid funds* (i.e. cash at bank and in hand and cash equivalents [e.g. investments held as current assets] less bank overdrafts and other borrowings repayable within one year of the accounting date).

The information in the SSAF is derived from the profit and loss account and opening and closing balance sheets, and its objective is, to quote from the standard's explanatory note:

'. . . to show the manner in which the operations of a company have been financed and in which its financial resources have been used and the format selected should be designed to achieve this objective. A funds statement does not purport to indicate the requirements of a business for capital nor the extent of seasonal peaks of stocks, debtors, etc.'

The precise form of the SSAF, as the above quotation indicates, is left to the discretion of the individual accountant. An appendix to the standard does, however, give three example statements for general guidance, and the following specimen statement is based on the first of those examples:

The Knotty Ash Treacle Co. Ltd
Source and Application of Funds Statement for the Year ended 31 July
1987

Source of funds

Profit before tax		62 890
Adjustments for items not involving the movement of funds:		
Depreciation		9 678
Total generated from operations		72 568

Funds from other sources

Issue of shares for cash	23 000	
Proceeds from sale of fixed assets	12 907	
		35 907
		108 475

Application of funds

Purchase of fixed assets	29 653	
Redemption of debentures	15 000	
Dividends paid	23 876	
Taxation paid	21 211	
		89 740
		18 735

Increase in working capital

Increase in stocks		13 394	
Increase in debtors		15 098	
Increase in creditors – excluding taxation and proposed dividends		(9 800)	
Movement in net liquid funds:			
Increase (decrease) in:			
Cash and bank balances	145		
Short-term investments	(102)		
		43	
			18 735

NB   In practice, comparative figures for the previous year would be given.

In addition to providing example statements, SSAP 10 includes a number of recommendations as to the way various matters should be treated, as follows:

1.   The statement should distinguish the use of funds for the purchase of fixed assets from funds used in increasing the working capital.

2. A minimum of 'netting off' should take place, e.g. the sale of one building and the purchase of another should generally be kept separate.

3. Whilst figures from which the SSAF are constructed should generally be identifiable in the P&L account, balance sheet and related notes, details should be given in cases where any adjustments to those published figures are necessary.

4. The SSAF for companies with subsidiaries should be based on the group accounts, and should reflect purchases or disposals of subsidiaries either as (a) separate items or (b) by reflecting the effects on the separate assets and liabilities dealt with in the statement. This is explained in more detail later in the chapter.

5. In addition to disclosing the profit/loss and the 'non-cash' adjustments (e.g. depreciation), the following should also be shown (where material):

   (a) dividends paid;*
   (b) acquisitions and disposals of fixed and other non-current assets (e.g. investments);
   (c) funds raised by increasing (or expended in repaying or redeeming) medium or long-term loans or the issued share capital of the company;
   (d) increase or decrease in working capital subdivided into its components, and movements in net liquid funds.

Taxation paid, whilst not specifically mentioned in the standard, is shown as an application of funds in the example statement, rather than as part of the 'working capital' changes.

ALTERNATIVE LAYOUTS

Whilst the standard is not prescriptive in the form of layout to be adopted, most companies follow the example statement referred to earlier. The most commonly used alternative presentation is one which places greater emphasis on the changes in the net liquid funds, as can be seen by using the same figures as in the 'Knotty Ash Treacle Co. Ltd' example in the previous section:

Source of funds
(same as previous example)   108 475

Application of funds

Purchase of fixed assets	29 653	
Redemption of debentures	15 000	
Dividends paid	23 876	
Taxation paid	21 211	
Increase in working capital:		
Increase in stocks	13 394	
Increase in debtors	15 098	
Increase in creditors (excluding tax		
and dividends)	(9 800)	
		18 692
		108 432
		43

Increase in net liquid funds

Increase (decrease) in:	145	
Cash and bank balances		
Short-term investments	(102)	
		43

This format should be used where questions specifically ask for an
explanation of the movements in the cash and bank balances in the
period. In other cases, it is best to follow the previous example.

METHODOLOGY

There is no substitute for practice in preparing funds flow statements, and students should take every opportunity to attempt as many questions as possible. The following is a useful guide to the best way to proceed:

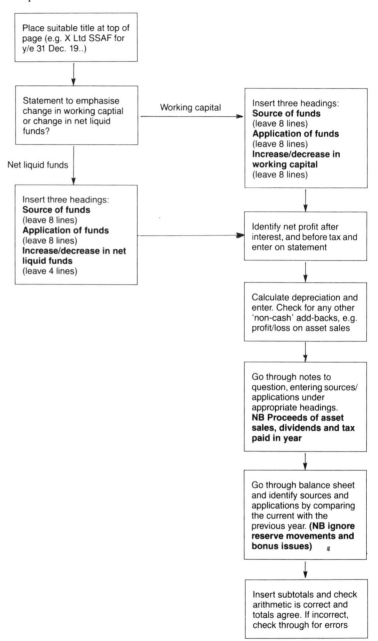

COMPANIES WITH SUBSIDIARIES

As mentioned earlier, the standard allows two ways of disclosing the purchase or disposal of subsidiaries, either by disclosure as separate items or by reflecting the effects on the separate assets and liabilities dealt with in the statement. In the latter case, the acquisition of a subsidiary company would be dealt with as an application of funds in acquiring the fixed assets (including goodwill) of that subsidiary and as a change in working capital. In either case, a footnote is normally provided which summarises the effects of the acquisition and disposal, indicating, in the case of an acquisition, how much of the purchase price has been discharged in cash and how much by the issue of shares.

INTERPRETATION OF THE STATEMENT

Questions often require not only the preparation of an SSAF but also comment upon its contents. The following matters should be considered when making an analytical review of the statement:

1. The relationship between source and application of funds and the reasons for any imbalance.
2. The strengths and weaknesses of the company's working capital.
3. The ways in which the funds have been raised, and the balance between 'internal funding' (e.g. net profit) and 'external' funding (e.g. issues of debentures).
4. The uses made of the funds which were raised.
5. Movements in the net liquid funds during the year.
6. Effect on gearing levels due to loan issues or repayments.
7. Relationship of profit/dividend (or loss/dividend).
8. Signs of over-trading (i.e. company expansion without adequate finance).
9. Trends of figures, by reference to previous years' statements.

C USEFUL APPLIED MATERIALS

Two extracts from the annual reports of public limited companies, showing different ways of presenting the statement, are reproduced in Figs 8.1 and 8.2.

Figure 8.1 Bardon Hill Group plc; statement of source and application of funds

Source & Application of Funds

	1986 £'000	1986 £'000	1985 £'000	1985 £'000
Source of funds				
Profit of the group before taxation		4,669		4,294
Adjustments for items not involving the movement of funds:				
Depreciation	2,920		2,369	
Share of loss of related company	113		43	
Profit on sale of fixed assets	(383)	2,650	(456)	1,956
Total generated from operations		7,319		6,250
Funds from other sources				
Sales of fixed assets	1,465		1,177	
Increase in creditors: amounts falling due after more than one year	6,246		597	
Issue of ordinary shares	1,490		—	
Issue of loan notes	511	9,712	—	1,774
		17,031		8,024
Application of funds				
Purchase of subsidiary companies	8,817		624	
Purchase of fixed assets	4,836		5,288	
Dividends paid	912		786	
Taxation	1,361		387	
Investment in related company	20	15,946	—	7,085
		1,085		939
Movements in working capital				
Stock		(871)		(613)
Investments		(574)		217
Debtors		(48)		629
Creditors: amounts falling due within one year		547		1,190
Cash		558		—
Bank overdrafts		1,473		(484)
		1,085		939

The effects on the source and application of funds of the acquisition of new businesses during the year are as follows:

	1986 £'000	1985 £'000
Assets acquired:		
Tangible fixed assets	5,868	348
Stock	1,427	63
Debtors	4,539	52
Cash at bank	380	31
Creditors including bank overdrafts and loans	(5,429)	(108)
Deferred taxation	(231)	(121)
Goodwill	2,263	359
	8,817	624
Discharged by:		
Cash (including expenses)	6,816	624
Issue of loan notes	511	—
Issue of ordinary shares	1,490	—
	8,817	624

Figure 8.2 Marks and Spencer plc; statement of source and application of funds

CONSOLIDATED SOURCE AND APPLICATION OF FUNDS

FOR THE YEAR ENDED 31 MARCH 1986

	1986 £m	1985 £m
Cash and short-term funds at 1 April 1985	101·1	95·2
Source of funds		
Arising from trading		
Profit on ordinary activities before taxation	365·8	304·1
Depreciation	52·7	44·7
Sales of fixed assets	5·5	2·4
	424·0	351·2
From other sources		
Shares issued under employees' share schemes	6·9	6·4
	532·0	452·8
Application of funds		
Payment of dividends	94·3	83·9
Payment of taxation	119·7	94·1
Purchase of fixed assets	158·9	121·8
Miscellaneous	(0·2)	2·3
Increase in net assets of financial activities excluding taxation (see below)	5·9	7·9
	378·6	310·0
Increase/(decrease) in working capital		
Stock	5·6	35·6
Debtors	47·5	·6
Creditors under one year (excluding taxation and dividends)	(34·6)	(18·7)
Group relief payable to financial activities	(5·0)	24·0
Creditors over one year	3·2	·2
	16·7	41·7
	395·3	351·7
Cash and short-term funds at 31 March 1986	136·7	101·1

Cash and short-term funds comprise cash at bank and in hand and current asset investments less bank loans and overdrafts.

Increase in net assets of financial activities		
Purchase of assets for finance leasing	·1	28·6
Capital repayments on leases	(20·6)	(13·9)
	(20·5)	14·7
Increase in fixed assets	4·0	—
Increase in trade debtors	84·2	4·2
Increase/(decrease) in group relief receivable	5·0	(24·0)
(Increase)/decrease in bank loans and overdrafts	(73·1)	9·4
Increase in other working capital	6·3	3·6
Net movement	5·9	7·9

1 The practice of providing a source and application of funds statement as a part of audited accounts is now well established.

Required:

(a) What purpose is such a statement intended to serve? Is it effective in providing information for its users? How is it constructed and what headings and details are normally included and why? What are its relationships to the other statements which make up the audited accounts?

(15 marks)

(b) Contrast the treatment of the following items in a source and application of funds statement with their treatment in a profit and loss account:

(i) Sales of fixed assets, and
(ii) Ordinary share dividends.

(5 marks)
(Total 20 marks)
(The Institute of Chartered Secretaries and Administrators, Dec. 1985)

2 Some of the transactions of Nidd plc during the year ended 30 June Year 5 were as follows:

(1) Sold plant and machinery costing £10 000 (accumulated depreciation £9 000) for £2 000.
(2) Paid the dividend proposed at 30 June Year 4 £3 000; paid an interim dividend of £1 000, and proposed a final dividend for the year ended 30 June Year 5 of £4 000.
(3) Issued 100 000 £1 Ordinary Shares at a premium of 20 pence per share. Share issue expenses (debited to share premium account) amounted to £750.
(4) Sold half the company's short-term investments for £4 000 (cost £3 500). No other short-term investments were either bought or sold during the year.
(5) Purchased all the shares in Aire plc (a company operating in the same industry) for £12 000 in cash.

Required:

(i) Outline what you consider to be the main functions of source and application of funds statements in financial reporting.
(Subtotal 6 marks)

(ii) Briefly explain how each of the above transactions should be dealt with in a funds statement prepared in accordance with SSAP 10. Include any alternative treatments.
(Subtotal 12 marks)
(Total 18 marks)
(LCCI – Higher, Spring 1985)

3 The following information is provided for the Shelton Manufacturing Co. Ltd.

(i)

Balance sheet as at 30 June

	1985 (£)	1984 (£)
Capital and liabilities		
Ordinary share capital (£1 ordinary shares)	100 000	100 000
Reserves	52 500	44 000
	152 500	144 000
14 per cent bank loan	60 000	—
Creditors and accruals	24 000	15 000
Taxation payable 31 March	15 100	10 000
Proposed dividend	15 000	15 000
	£266 600	£184 000
Assets		
Plant and machinery at cost	200 000	100 000
Less: Accumulated depreciation	75 000	40 000
	125 000	60 000
Freehold property at cost	25 000	25 000
Investments at cost	—	11 000
Stock and work in progress	74 000	43 000
Debtors and prepayments	41 000	28 000
Cash and bank balance	1 600	17 000
	£266 600	£184 000

(ii)

Profit and Loss account extracts
year to 30 June 1985

	(£)
Profit from ordinary activities	42 000
Less: Interest payable	8 400
Profit before tax	33 600
Less: Taxation	13 600
Profit before extraordinary item	20 000
Profit arising from sale of investments (less tax £1 500)	3 500
Profit available for appropriation	23 500
Less: Proposed dividend	15 000
Retained profit for the year	£8 500

(iii) The company purchased additional plant, costing £100 000, in the autumn of 1984. The plant became fully operational on 1 January 1985 and this resulted in profits from ordinary activities, in the second half of the financial year to 30 June 1985, which were twice as high as in the previous six months.

(iv) The bank loan is secured on the freehold property. The advance was made on 1 July 1984 and is repayable by four quarterly instalments commencing 30 September 1985. Interest is payable at the end of each quarter.

(v) The directors estimate that the freehold property, which is essential to the business, would fetch £75 000 on the open market.

(vi) The proposed dividend is usually paid within two weeks of the annual general meeting which is held at the beginning of March.

(vii) The investments were sold in December 1984.

The directors estimate that, during the year to 30 June 1986:

(i) Profits from ordinary activities will accrue at the same rate as in the second half of the year to 30 June 1985, and this will give rise to a tax liability of £18 000 for the full year.

(iii) The depreciation charge will be the same as in the previous year.

(iii) Changes in the system of stock control will enable the level of investment in stock and work in progress to be reduced to £65 000.

(iv) The levels of debtors and creditors will remain approximately the same.

(v) Interest payable on the bank loan will amount to £5 250, and the directors again propose to pay a dividend of £15 000.

Required:

(**a**) A discussion of past performance based on:
- (i) A statement of source and application of funds for the year to 30 June 1985.
- (ii) The pre-tax rate of return on shareholders' equity.
- (iii) The liquidity ratio at 30 June 1985. (15 marks)

(**b**) A discussion, so far as the information permits, of future prospects based on:
- (i) An estimated source and application of funds for the year to 30 June 1986.
- (ii) The estimated pre-tax rate of return on shareholders' equity.
- (iii) The estimated liquidity ratio at 30 June 1986. (15 marks)

Notes:
1. Ignore advance corporation tax.
2. For the purpose of calculating the rate of return, shareholders' equity is defined as share capital plus reserves at the beginning of the year.
3. You may assume that the bank has agreed to provide overdraft facilities to meet any estimated cash deficiency

during the year to 30 June 1986. Interest payable on any overdraft needed may be ignored.

(Total marks for question – 30)

(The Institute of Bankers, Sept. 1985)

E ANSWERS

1(a) To quote from SSAP 10, a statement of source and application of funds shows 'the manner in which the operations of a company have been financed and in which its financial resources have been used'. It acts as an important link between the profit and loss account and the opening and closing balance sheets as well as showing how the profit generated and any additional funds received in the year have been applied as actual spending or retentions for working capital, etc.

It is constructed from the information contained within the opening and closing balance sheets, as well as the P&L account for the current year. Whilst examples of formats for the source and application of funds statement are given in the standard, they are not prescriptive, and variations are divided primarily between those statements which concentrate on the change in working capital in the year, and those which show the change in net liquid funds between the beginning and end of the year (see examples given within the chapter).

1(b)

(i) Sales of fixed assets are given the following treatment:

In the P&L account, the profit or loss (i.e. over-or under-depreciation in previous years) is credited or debited within the account. If the profit or loss is *extraordinary* then it would be disclosed separately in accordance with SSAP 6 (see Ch. 10).

In the source and application of funds statement, only the proceeds of sale are treated as a source of funds, whilst the amount of profit or loss charged in the profit and loss account would be written back against net profit (or net loss) as an 'item not involving the movement of funds'.

(ii) Ordinary share dividends are treated as follows:

In the P&L account, ordinary share dividends both paid and proposed are shown as appropriations of profit.

In the source and application of funds statement, only the dividends paid in the year are included as applications of funds.

2(i) See answer to **1(a)** above.

2(ii)

(1) Profit on sale = (£2 000 − Net book value of £1 000) = £1 000, which will be deducted from net profit (or added to net loss) as an item not involving the movement of funds. The proceeds of sale, £2 000, are shown as a source of funds.

(2) The dividends paid in the year, £3 000 + £1 000 = £4 000, are shown as applications of funds in the statement.

(3) The standard recommends that a minimum of 'netting off' should take place, so the gross proceeds of the issue, £120 000, should be shown as a source of funds, whilst the £750 expenses should be shown as an application.

(4) The proceeds of sale of the short-term investments (£4 000) can be shown as a source of funds. Alternatively, the change in the asset can be treated as a working capital item, and shown separately in that section of the statement.

(5) Either show the £120 000 as an application of funds, with a footnote being provided giving a breakdown of the individual assets and liabilities acquired, or disclose it by reflecting the effects on the separate assets and liabilities within the statement.

3(a) The following is the source and application of funds statement of the Shelton Manufacturing Co. Ltd for the year ended 30 June 1985:

Source and Application of Funds Statement for the Year ended 30 June 1985

Source of funds		
Profit from ordinary activities, before tax		42 000
Less: interest payable		8 400
		33 600
Adjustments for items not involving the movement of funds:		
Depreciation (75 000 − 40 000)		35 000
Total generated from operations		68 600
Funds from other sources		
Bank loan received	60 000	
Proceeds from sale of investments	16 000	
(11 000 − 3 500 + 1 500)		
		76 000
		144 600
Application of funds		
Purchase of plant	100 000	
Dividends paid	15 000	
Taxation paid	10 000	
		125 000
		19 600
Increase in working capital		
Increase in stocks	31 000	
Increase in debtors	13 000	
Increase in creditors – excluding taxation and proposed dividends	(9 000)	
Movement in net liquid funds:		
Decrease in:		
Cash and bank balances	(15 400)	
		19 600

The pre-tax return on shareholders' equity at 30 June 1985 was as follows:

$$\frac{33\ 600}{144\ 000} \times \frac{100}{1} = 23.3 \text{ per cent}$$

The liquidity ratio at 30 June 1985 was:

$(41\ 000 + 1\ 600) : (60\ 000 + 24\ 000 + 15\ 100 + 15\ 000) = 42\ 600 : 114\ 100 = 0.37 : 1$

The past performance as disclosed by the above indicates that the company was in an unstable financial position, arising from high bank borrowings, and seemingly excessive stock levels. The liquidity ratio reveals that the company had only 37p of liquid assets to meet each £1 of current liabilities. However, the source and application of funds statement shows that the company is investing for the future by applying £100 000 towards the purchase of fixed assets.

3(b) The company's source and application of funds statement for the year ended 30 June 1986 is shown below:

Source and Application of Funds Statement for the Year ended 30 June 1986

Source of funds		
Profit from ordinary activities, before tax		56 000
Less: Interest payable		5 250
		50 750
Adjustments for items not involving the movement of funds:		
Depreciation (75 000 − 40 000)		35 000
Total generated from operations		85 750
Application of funds		
Dividends paid	15 000	
Taxation paid	15 100	
		30 100
		55 650
Increase in working capital		
Decrease in stocks	(9 000)	
Movement in net liquid funds:		
Decrease in:		
Cash and bank balances	60 000	
Decrease in bank loan	4 650	
		55 650

The pre-tax return on shareholders' equity at 30 June 1986 was as follows:

$$\frac{50\ 750}{152\ 000} \times \frac{100}{1} = 33 \text{ per cent}$$

The liquidity ratio at 30 June 1986 was:

$$(41\ 000 + 6\ 250):(24\ 000 + 18\ 000 + 15\ 000) = 47\ 250:$$
$$57\ 000 = 0.8:1$$

The predicted results for the year ended 30 June 1986 show a distinct improvement over those for the previous year. Both the return on shareholders' equity and the liquidity ratio are strengthened, and the source and application of funds statement indicates that the company is generating greater funds from profits, and that it is succeeding in reducing stock levels. The bank loan will be repaid largely out of funds internally generated by the company.

F   A STEP FURTHER

The following references are given for the purpose of further study:

G. H. Black, *Financial Accounting* (Woodhead-Faulkner). Ch. 9. *Selected Accounting Standards – Interpretation Problems Explained* (ICAEW), pp. 55–76.

Chapter 9

Taxation: Value added tax; the imputation system; deferred taxation

SSAPs 5, 8 and 15

A GETTING STARTED

As Benjamin Franklin said, 'In this world nothing is certain but death and taxes', and there is little which is as perennially certain for the accountancy student as the requirement to have a knowledge of the ways in which taxation is treated in the financial statements.

In this chapter, we start with one of the shortest SSAPs (SSAP 5: *Accounting for Value Added Tax*) and end with one of the longest (SSAP 15: *Accounting for Deferred Taxation*). In between, we look at SSAP 8, concerned with 'the treatment of taxation under the imputation system in the accounts of companies'. The word *imputation* is derived from the Latin *imputare*, meaning *to bring into the reckoning or enter into the account*.

Examination questions on the three taxation standards tend to concentrate on knowledge of:

1. The correct presentation of matters appertaining to taxation, both in the bookkeeping system and the financial statements.
2. The underlying reasons *why* particular treatments are adopted.

B ESSENTIAL PRINCIPLES

SSAP 5: *ACCOUNTING FOR VALUE ADDED TAX*

Value added tax (VAT) is a system of taxation whereby the tax is collected at each stage of the production and distribution chain (i.e. as *value* is *added* to the product) but is eventually borne by the final consumer. The trader acts, therefore, as a tax collector, accounting for VAT output tax (the VAT charged to customers on sales) and VAT input tax (the VAT charged by his suppliers on purchases, expenses, etc.), and either paying or receiving the balance at intervals to or from the taxation authorities (HM Customs and Excise in the UK), as follows:

If VAT output tax exceeds VAT input tax: Difference paid to tax authority
If VAT input tax exceeds VAT output tax: Difference received from tax authority

Note that only those traders who are *registered* for VAT purposes are allowed to charge VAT on their supplies and offset VAT suffered on their purchases and expenses. Registration is compulsory in the UK for traders who have an annual turnover which exceeds a prescribed amount (£20 500 at the time of writing). It is possible for certain businesses to opt for voluntary registration, even though their turnover is below that figure. This may prove beneficial to businesses with a small turnover whose customers are mainly registered traders.

Non-registered businesses, therefore, *suffer* the VAT input tax, i.e. the cost of goods and services will increase, as will the cost of fixed assets. No separate VAT accounting records need to be kept, and the financial statements will include all relevant amounts at their 'VAT-inclusive' prices.

Exempted activities	Whilst there are only two rates of VAT, standard rate (15 per cent) and zero rate (0 per cent), there are certain activities, such as insurance and banking services, which are treated as *exempt* from VAT. This means simply that whilst no VAT need be added to (e.g.) insurance premiums and bank charges, the insurance companies and banks cannot, in most circumstances, reclaim VAT on inputs relating to the provision of those exempted activities.
Non-deductible inputs*	Not all VAT input tax can be offset against output tax. Examples include the VAT paid on motor cars and on most business entertaining. Such 'irrecoverable' VAT must be included in the amounts to be disclosed in the published accounts where practicable and material.
Amounts due to or from the revenue authorities	At the end of the accounting period, the amount due to or from the revenue authorities should be included as part of debtors or creditors, and will not normally require separate disclosure.
Capital commitments	The estimated amount of capital commitments disclosed in a company's final accounts (in accordance with the Companies Act 1985) should include the amount, if any, of irrecoverable VAT.
Turnover*	Turnover shown in the P&L account should exclude VAT on taxable outputs. If it is desired to show the *gross* turnover then the VAT relevant to that turnover should be shown as a deduction.

Only those paragraphs marked * above are contained within the
SSAP. The remainder of the section has been taken from the
'explanatory note to the standard', or from other sources.

SUMMARY OF SSAP 5

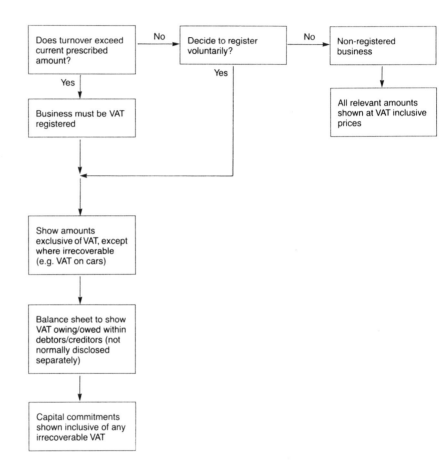

SSAP 8: *THE TREATMENT OF TAXATION UNDER THE IMPUTATION SYSTEM IN THE ACCOUNTS OF COMPANIES*

The imputation system of corporation tax refers to the method of
taxation whereby the whole of a company's taxable profit, regardless
of the proportion of that profit which is distributed by way of
dividend, is subject to a corporation tax charge.

If a company pays a dividend, it must make an advance payment
of corporation tax (ACT) to the tax authorities. The ACT is normally
able to be offset against the company's total liability on its income
(but not any capital gains) for the same accounting period. The
resultant net amount due is known as the *mainstream* corporation tax.

Note that the amount of ACT which can be offset against the total liability is restricted to a percentage equal to the current income tax rate.

The payment dates for ACT and the mainstream tax liabilities are as follows:

- ACT – within 14 days of the end of the calendar quarter in which dividends have been paid;
- Mainstream tax – either:
    1. (Companies incorporated prior to 1 April 1965):
       Payable on 1 January following the end of the tax year in which their accounting period ended. Companies which have changed their accounting date since 1965 preserve the same time gap as would have originally applied under this rule.
    2. (Companies incorporated on or after 1 April 1965):
       Payable 9 months after the end of the company's account period.

If all or part of the ACT is *unrelieved* against the total tax liability, then the unrelieved ACT can be carried back and set against the corporation tax liability of accounting periods commencing in the previous 6 years, or carried forward without time limit.

The following is a simple example showing the relationship between ACT and total corporation tax liability. A company, incorporated in 1980, had taxable profits of £900 000 for the year ended 31 January 1987. The company paid a dividend of £280 000 in November 1986. Assume a corporation tax rate of 40 per cent, an income tax rate of 30 per cent and an ACT rate of 3/7.

	£
Profits chargeable to corporation tax	900 000
Corporation tax payable (40 per cent × £900 000)	360 000
ACT* on dividend (3/7 × £280 000)	120 000
(*Maximum ACT set-off 30 per cent × £900 000 = £270 000*)	
Mainstream corporation tax payable†	240 000

Notes:
*Payable within 14 days of 31 December 1986.
†Payable on 1 November 1987.

ACCOUNTING PROBLEMS

The main accounting problems related to the imputation system are listed in the 'explanatory note' to the standard as follows:

(a) the treatment in the P&L account of outgoing dividends and the related ACT;

(b) determining the recoverability of ACT;

(c) the treatment of irrecoverable ACT and of unrelieved overseas tax arising from the payment or proposed payment of dividends;

(d) the treatment of franked investment income;

(e) the treatment in the balance sheet of taxation liabilities, recoverable ACT and dividends.

Dividends and related ACT	As stated earlier, the company must pay ACT whenever it pays a dividend. In the P&L appropriation account, the dividend will be shown *exclusive* of ACT, whilst the related ACT will be shown as part of the tax on the company's profits. In this way, the full corporation tax charge is shown, not merely the mainstream tax liability.
Recoverability of ACT	ACT is recovered primarily by being set off against the corporation tax on the income of the year in which the related dividend is made. As explained earlier, unrelieved ACT can be carried back over the previous 6 years, or carried forward without time limit. Difficulties arise for those companies which have insufficient taxable income, as the ACT paid is not able to be offset. For accounting purposes, it is necessary to decide whether recovery of the ACT is *reasonably certain and foreseeable*, or whether it should be written off in the P&L account. Although relief remains available indefinitely, it is prudent to consider only the immediate position and the foreseeable future. There are additional considerations to be made where a *deferred taxation account* is maintained. These will be discussed later in the chapter (see SSAP 15: *Accounting for Deferred Tax*).
Irrecoverable ACT and unrelieved overseas tax	If ACT is deemed to be irrecoverable (see previous section), it should be written off in the P&L account in which the related dividend is shown. Two possible treatments are discussed in the explanatory note to the standard:

1. Treating the irrecoverable ACT as part of the tax charge for the year; or
2. Treating the irrecoverable ACT in the same way as the dividend itself, i.e. as an appropriation of profits.

The first alternative is preferred, as unrelieved ACT constitutes tax upon the company or group, as opposed to tax upon the shareholders, and is *not* an appropriation of profits. Note that the amount of any irrecoverable ACT should be separately disclosed in the financial statements, if material.

In some circumstances, tax paid on overseas income may be unrelieved against that paid on UK income. In such cases, the accounting treatment is similar to that applied to irrecoverable ACT.

Franked investment income	Many companies own shares in other companies on which they receive dividends. The paying company accounts for ACT in the usual way, the dividend and related ACT being referred to by the recipient company as *franked investment income* (FII). 'Franked' in this context means simply that the appropriate tax has been (or will be) rendered to the relevant tax authorities by the paying company. The company receiving FII is able to offset the related ACT against any ACT due when it pays its own dividends.

Two possible methods of showing the FII in the P&L account are suggested:

1. Crediting the cash received or receivable (i.e. excluding the ACT); or
2. Crediting the total FII, including the related ACT. The ACT on FII is included as part of the year's tax charge.

The first method was rejected as it would involve treating the income either as an item of profit before taxation, or as an addition to profit after taxation, both of which are open to objection.

The second method is the standard accounting practice, as it allows, to quote from the explanatory foreword, 'recognition of the income both at the pre-tax and at the after-tax stage in a way which is consistent with other elements of profit'.

Summary of profit and loss account treatment.

The following should be included in the taxation charge, and, where material, should be disclosed separately:

(a) the amount of the UK corporation tax specifying:
   (i) the charge for corporation tax on the income of the year (showing transfers between the deferred tax account and the P&L account, where material – see SSAP 15);
   (ii) tax attributable to franked investment income;
   (iii) irrecoverable ACT;
   (iv) the relief for overseas taxation;
(b) the total overseas taxation, relieved and unrelieved, specifying that part of the unrelieved overseas taxation which arises from the payment or proposed payment of dividends.

Dividends paid (and/or proposed) should exclude the related ACT, whilst dividends received should *include* the related ACT.

Balance sheet treatment

As explained earlier, the payment dates for the mainstream corporation tax depend upon the date of the company's formation. For many companies, there will be only a current liability shown on the balance sheet, i.e. the mainstream corporation tax due 9 months from the balance sheet date. For 'pre-1965' companies, not only will there be a current liability, but there will also be a 'Creditor falling due after more than one year', being the mainstream corporation tax due for the current accounting year.

Proposed dividends should be shown *without* the addition of the related ACT. The ACT (whether recoverable or irrecoverable) is shown as a current liability. If the ACT is regarded as being recoverable, it should be deducted from the deferred tax account (see SSAP 15), if available. If there is no deferred tax account, the recoverable ACT should be shown as a deferred asset.

The way in which an actual company shows taxation matters in its annual accounts is contained in Section C: Useful Applied Materials.

SUMMARY OF SSAP 8

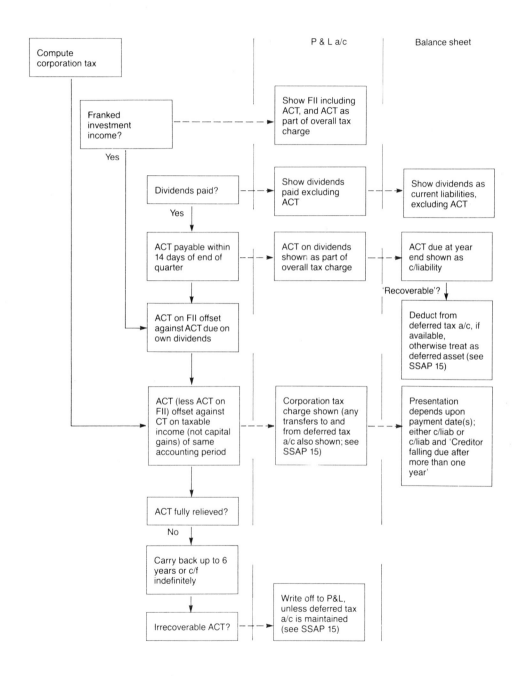

SSAP 15: *ACCOUNTING FOR DEFERRED TAX*

This statement, which does not apply to immaterial items, relates to the problems which arise when the tax payable on the profits of a particular period bears little relation to the income and expenditure appearing in the financial statements for that period. There are two main reasons for such an imbalance.

1. Permanent differences

Certain types of income are tax free (dividends and other distributions from UK companies), and certain types of expenditure are not able to be offset against taxable profits (e.g. depreciation, most business entertainment). These give rise to *permanent* differences between taxable and accounting profits. Permanent differences also arise where there are tax allowances or charges with no corresponding amount in the financial statements.

As these differences will not be reversed in future years, there is no requirement to consider them in relation to a deferred tax provision.

2. Timing differences

Certain items are included in the financial statements of one period, but treated in a different period for taxation purposes (e.g. interest received, which is treated on an 'accruals' basis for the annual accounts, but on a 'cash' basis when tax is being computed). This disparity of treatment gives rise to *timing* differences.

The standard defines deferred tax as 'the tax attributable to timing differences'.

BASIS OF PROVISION

The 'explanatory note' to the standard lists three principal bases for computing deferred tax.

1. 'Nil provision' or 'flow through' basis

This is based on the principle that only the tax payable in respect of a period should be charged in that period, and therefore no provision for deferred tax need be made. Those who argue in favour of this basis state that as tax liability arises on taxable profits, not accounting profits, it is necessary to provide for tax only on taxable profits. In addition, they argue that any tax liability arising on timing differences will depend upon the incidence of future taxable profits and may therefore be difficult to quantify.

2. 'Full provision' basis

As its name implies, this is the opposite of the 'nil provision basis', as it is based on the principle that the tax effects (*whether current or deferred*) of *all* transactions of the period should be reflected in the financial statements for that period.

3. 'Partial provision' basis

This is a more pragmatic approach than the other two bases, as it requires that deferred tax be accounted for only when it is likely that such a liability will crystallise. It recognises that, for a going concern, there is likely to be a 'hard core' of timing differences which are being permanently deferred, as one timing difference is replaced by another before it crystallises.

Bases (1) and (2) above have the advantage that the amounts involved can be precisely quantified, but their disadvantage is that they may lead to a purely arithmetical approach being adopted, leading to a disregard of the likely tax effects of the transactions. Basis (3) is considered preferable, as it requires an assessment of the potential liability which would result if and when the timing differences crystallise.

METHODS OF COMPUTATION

Two principal methods exist.

1. The deferral method

This method uses the tax rates current *when the differences arise*, i.e. no adjustments are made subsequently if tax rates change. Advocates of the deferral method argue that the mere fact of a change in tax rates does not indicate the potential amount of tax payable or recoverable relating to the timing differences. Any balance on the deferred tax account will therefore be shown on the balance sheet as a deferred tax credit or charge rather than as an asset or liability.

2. The liability method

Under this method, the deferred tax provisions are calculated at the rate at which it is estimated that the tax will be paid (or recovered) when the timing differences reverse. As tax rates change, therefore, the provision will be recalculated.

The standard favours the liability method as being consistent with the 'partial provision' basis outlined earlier.

STANDARD ACCOUNTING PRACTICE

The standard comprises twenty-two paragraphs, divided into 'General', 'Profit and loss account', 'Balance sheet' and 'Groups', of which the following is a summary.

General

Deferred tax should be computed under the liability method, and accounted for only to the extent that it is probable that an asset or liability will crystallise. 'Reasonable assumptions' should be used to decide on the likelihood of crystallisation, taking into account all relevant information, including financial plans or projections. A prudent approach should be adopted, particularly where there is a high degree of uncertainty over future prospects.

Profit and loss account

The amount of deferred tax relating to the company's ordinary activities should be shown as part of the tax on profit or loss on ordinary activities for the year, either on the face of the P&L account, or as a note to it. Any deferred tax relates to *extraordinary* activities (see SSAP 6) should be shown separately as part of the tax on extraordinary items.

The amount of any *unprovided* deferred tax in respect of the period should be shown as a note, analysed into its major components.

Adjustments to deferred tax arising from a change in tax rates and allowances should be disclosed separately as part of the tax charge for the year, but the effect of changes in the basis of taxation, or major changes in government fiscal policy should be treated as an extraordinary item where material.

Balance sheet

The deferred tax balance should be disclosed on the balance sheet or notes, and a note should be given of any transfers to or from the account.

Where amounts of deferred tax arise which relate to movements on reserves (e.g. an asset revaluation reserve), the amounts transferred to or from the deferred tax account should be shown separately as part of such movements.

The total amount of any unprovided deferred tax should be shown by way of note, analysed into its major components.

Deferred tax provisions should be shown in the balance sheet under the heading 'Provision for liabilities and charges'. Any deferred tax carried forward as an asset should be included under the heading 'Prepayments and accrued income'.

Groups

A company which is a member of a group should take into account group relief which may be available when accounting for deferred tax.

DEFERRED TAX AND ACT

Where a company has a deferred tax account, any unrelieved ACT (see SSAP 8) can be offset against it, except for any part of the deferred tax which represents deferred chargeable gains. In the absence of a deferred tax account, any ACT recoverable should be shown as a deferred asset.

C USEFUL APPLIED MATERIALS

The following extracts from the published annual report of Associated British Foods plc (Figs 9.1–9.5) show how that company treats the various taxation items appearing in its financial statements.

Figure 9.1 Associated British Foods plc; treatment of taxation in the profit and loss account

Consolidated profit and loss account

	Note	For the year ended 29 March 1986 £ million	For the year ended 30 March 1985 £ million
Turnover	1	**3,129.2**	2,930.6
Trading surplus	2	**131.6**	114.8
Interest payable	4	**7.5**	6.0
Group profit		**124.1**	108.8
Investment income	5	**39.4**	23.5
Profit on ordinary activities before taxation	1	**163.5**	132.3
Taxation on profit on ordinary activities	6	**63.2**	51.4
Profit on ordinary activities after taxation		**100.3**	80.9
Minority interests		**2.0**	2.0
Profit on ordinary activities attributable to the company		**98.3**	78.9
Extraordinary items	7	**13.5**	10.8
Profit for the financial year		**111.8**	89.7
Dividends of Associated British Foods plc	8	**24.3**	21.6
Retained profits	19	**87,5**	68.1
Earnings per share before extraordinary items	9	**24.7p**	19.8p
Reserves	19		
Previous balances		**821.2**	766.3
Retained profits		**87.5**	68.1
Other movements on reserves		**(11.5)**	(13.2)
Balances		**897.2**	821.2

Figure 9.2 Associated British Foods plc; treatment of taxation in the balance sheet

Consolidated balance sheet

	Note	As at 29 March 1986 £ million	As at 30 March 1985 £ million
Fixed assets			
Tangible assets	10	696.1	636.7
Investments	11	6.1	6.4
		702.2	643.1
Current assets			
Stocks	13	275.2	244.9
Debtors	14	188.7	176.6
Investments	15	292.4	259.3
Cash at bank and in hand		43.1	49.7
		799.4	730.5
Creditors amounts falling due within one year	16	521.8	451.0
Net current assets		277.6	279.5
Total assets less current liabilities		979.8	922.6
Creditors amounts falling due after one year	16	34.5	44.4
Provision for liabilities and charges	6	13.3	20.2
		932.0	858.0
Capital and reserves			
Called up share capital	18	20.9	20.9
Share premium account	19	39.9	39.9
Revaluation reserve	19	16.1	18.3
Other reserves	19	3.7	4.1
Profit and loss account	19	837.5	758.9
		918.1	842.1
Minority interests in subsidiaries		13.9	15.9
		932.0	858.0

Garry H. Weston Director

Wallace Monaghan Director

19 May 1986

Accounting policies

Deferred tax

Deferred tax represents corporation tax in respect of accelerated taxation allowances on capital expenditure and other timing differences to the extent that a liability is anticipated in the foreseeable future.

Figure 9.4 Associated British Foods plc; notes relating to taxation matters

Notes forming part of the accounts

6 Tax on profit on ordinary activities	1986 £ million	1985 £ million
The charge for the year is as follows		
United Kingdom—Corporation tax at 40 per cent. (1985 – 45 per cent.)	50.4	39.0
—Deferred tax	(7.1)	(1.1)
Overseas—Income tax	19.8	13.4
Deferred tax	0.1	0.1
	63.2	51.4

The provision for liabilities and charges represents deferred tax as follows:

	£ million
At 30 March 1985	20.2
Effect of currency changes	0.1
Released during the year	(7.0)
At 29 March 1986	13.3

The provision for deferred tax is in respect of accelerated capital allowances less other timing differences to the extent that a liability is anticipated. The full potential liability at 29 March 1986 was £82 million (1985—£85 million).

No provision has been made in these accounts for the additional tax which would be payable on the remittance to this country of the group's share of profits for the year retained by overseas subsidiaries.

7 Extraordinary items	1986 £ million	1985 £ million
Profits less losses on sales of property and investments	13.8	11.4
Profit on purchase of debenture stock for cancellation	—	0.1
Extraordinary profit	13.8	11.5
Tax on extraordinary profits	(0.3)	(0.2)
Attributable to minority interests	—	(0.5)
	13.5	10.8

Figure 9.5 Associated British Foods plc; notes relating to taxation matters (continued)

	1986 £ million	1985 £ million
8 Dividends of Associated British Foods plc		
Ordinary dividends		
First interim dividend of 1.9p per share (1985—1.7p) which together with the associated tax credit is equivalent to 2.71p per share (1985—2.43p)	7.6	6.8
Second interim dividend of 4.2p per share (1985—3.7p) which together with the associated tax credit is equivalent to 5.92p per share (1985—5.29p)	16.7	14.7
	24.3	21.5

The first interim dividend was paid in March 1986 on 398,424,377 shares (1985—398,424,377)
The second interim dividend will be paid in September 1986 on 398,424,377 shares (1985—398,424,377)
In addition, preference dividends of £40,000 (1985—£40,000) were paid in the year.

	Company 1986 £ million	Company 1985 £ million	Group 1986 £ million	Group 1985 £ million
16 Creditors				
Amounts falling due within one year				
Loans (see note 17)	71.6	15.7	73.6	42.2
Trade creditors	—	—	234.6	236.3
Taxation on profits	4.0	3.6	71.7	44.1
Other taxation and social security	0.1	0.1	16.0	14.3
Accruals and deferred income	0.7	0.7	100.7	91.8
Dividends	16.7	14.7	16.7	14.7
Due to holding company	0.5	0.5	8.5	7.6
Amount owed to group companies	13.0	29.8	—	—
	106.6	65.1	521.8	451.0
Amounts falling due after one year				
Loans (see note 17)	13.2	17.1	23.2	29.5
Taxation on profits	—	—	11.3	14.9
	13.2	17.1	34.5	44.4

D   RECENT EXAMINATION QUESTIONS

1   A company buys and sells goods some of which are:

(a)   subject to VAT at the standard rate of 15 per cent;

(b)   zero rated (those where no VAT is chargeable on sales but any VAT charged on purchases is recoverable);

(c)   exempt (those where no VAT is chargeable on sales and where any VAT charged is not recoverable).

You are given the following information:

1. The balance on the VAT account at the end of July was £4 700. This amount was paid on 30 August.
2. Purchases, including VAT at 15 per cent, during the quarter were:
   £69 000 for standard-rated goods;
   £6 900 for zero-rated goods;
   £2 300 for exempt goods.
3. Sales, not including VAT, during the quarter were:
   £100 000 for standard-rated goods;
   £10 000 for zero-rated goods;
   £5 000 for exempt goods.
4. All items purchased are for resale.

Required:
Write up a company's Value Added Tax account, sales account and purchases account in its ledger for the months of August, September and October, and show the balance outstanding on the VAT account at the end of the quarter. (10 marks)

(Institute of Cost and Management Accountants, Nov. 1985)

2
(**a**) Explain what you understand by the 'imputation system' of taxation. (3 marks)
(**b**) Set out, with an example, the rules for the payment and recovery of Advanced Corporation Tax (ACT). (10 marks)
(**c**) How would you treat the following transactions in the Profit and Loss Account and/or Balance Sheet of a public company according to the requirements of best accounting practice? The year end of the company is 31 December 19 . .
   (i) the Company receives a dividend of £24 500 on its investment in the shares of another company, on 30 September;
   (ii) the Company provides for a final dividend of £91 000 at the year end;
   (iii) the Company pays a half-year's interest on £100 000 of 12 per cent Debentures on 31 December. (12 marks)

(Total 25 marks)

(Association of Accounting Technicians, Dec. 1983)

3 How should you treat the following items when preparing financial statements in accordance with statements of standard accounting practice:

(**i**) franked investment income, (3 marks)
(**ii**) proposed dividends and the related advance corporation tax, (2 marks)
(**iii**) recoverable advance corporation tax, (2 marks)
(**iv**) irrecoverable advance corporation tax, (2 marks)
(**v**) value added output tax on turnover for a VAT registered trader, (2 marks)
(**vi**) irrecoverable value added input tax on a fixed asset, purchased by a VAT registered trader. (2 marks)

(**vii**) the receipt and payment of VAT to the Customs and Excise?

(2 marks)
(Total 15 marks)
(Chartered Association of Certified Accountants, Dec. 1985)

4 Lancaster Ltd was incorporated and commenced business in January 1982. The following trial balance was extracted from the books at 31 December 1982.

	£	£
Share capital (ordinary shares of £1 each)		1 000 000
Trade creditors		264 500
Operating profit		315 000
Royalties		90 000
Dividends received		7 000
Fixed assets at cost (purchased January 1982)	200 000	
Provision for depreciation at 31 December 1982		40 000
Stock, debtors and cash	1 469 500	
Interim dividend paid	35 000	
Advance corporation tax	12 000	
	£1 716 500	£1 716 500

The following additional information is provided:

1. Royalties consist of £65 000 received in cash and £25 000 outstanding at the year end.
2. The royalties outstanding give rise to a 'short-term' timing difference as defined by SSAP 15 entitled *Accounting for Deferred Taxation*.
3. The directors intend to claim a first year allowance of 100 per cent on the fixed assets purchased in January 1982. No provision for deferred taxation will be made in respect of the resulting timing difference as the directors are in possession of reliable evidence which supports their opinion that it will not reverse in the foreseeable future.
4. Corporation tax is payable at 52 per cent on *taxable* profits of £220 000.
5. The directors propose to pay a final dividend of 14p per share for 1982.

Required:
The profit and loss account of Lancaster Ltd for 1982 and balance sheet at 31 December 1982, not necessarily in a form for publication, but complying with the provisions in SSAP 15.

Note: Advance corporation tax should be taken as 3/7ths for the purpose of your calculations.

(20 marks)
(Institute of Bankers, April 1983)

Although question **1** is not specifically related to SSAP 5, it provides useful practice at understanding the basic bookkeeping underlying the VAT entries.

1 Value Added Tax Account

30 August	Cheque to Customs and Excise	4 700	31 July	Balance b/f		4 700
31 October	VAT on standard-rated purchases	9 000	31 October	VAT on standard-rated sales	15 000
	Balance c/d	6 000				
		19 700				19 700
			1 November	Balance b/d		6 000

Sales Account

	31 October	Invoices:	
		Standard rated	100 000
		Zero rated	10 000
		Exempt	5 000
			115 000

Purchases Account

31 October	Invoices:	
	Standard rated	
	(69 000 × 100/115)	60 000
	Zero rated	6 900
	Exempt	2 300
		69 200

2(a) The 'imputation system' of taxation refers to the method of taxation whereby the whole of a company's taxable profit, regardless of the proportion of that profit which is distributed by way of dividend, is subject to a corporation tax charge. If a company pays a dividend, it must pay an amount of advance corporation tax (ACT) to the tax authorities. This ACT is normally available to be offset against the company's total tax liability on its income (other than capital gains) for the same accounting period.

2(b) The rules for the payment and recovery of ACT are explained fully in the chapter.

2(c)

(i) The dividend received is franked investment income, and the amount to be credited in the P&L account is the total received, including the related ACT. Therefore, if ACT is 3/7, the amount to be credited is £24 500 + (3/7 × £24 500) = £35 000. The ACT is then shown as part of the year's tax charge.

(ii) The dividend as proposed will be shown net of ACT in the P&L account, with the related ACT being shown as a current liability in the balance sheet. The ACT recoverable is shown either as a deferred asset, or is deducted from the provision for deferred taxation if there is one.

(iii) The gross amount payable, £6 000, appears in the P&L account as an expense, and the income tax (not ACT!) is a current liability in the balance sheet, as it must be remitted to the tax authorities.

3(i) See answer to **2(c)** (i) above.

3(ii) See answer to **2(c)** (ii) above.

3(iii) See answer to **2(c)** (ii) above.

3(iv) Irrecoverable ACT should be included in the tax charge in the P&L account and, where material, disclosed separately.

3(v) Turnover should exclude VAT on taxable outputs.

3(vi) Irrecoverable VAT which has been paid on the purchase of a fixed asset by a VAT registered trader would be included in the cost of that asset in the financial statements.

3(vii) The receipt or payment of VAT to the Customs and Excise is recorded in a VAT account in the nominal ledger. Any amounts owing or owed at the end of the financial year would be included within creditors or debtors on the balance sheet, and will not normally require separate disclosure.

4

Lancaster Ltd

Profit and Loss Account for the Year ended 31 December 1982

Operating profit			315 000
Royalties			90 000
Dividends received (including tax credit)			10 000
Net profit before taxation			415 000
Transfer to provision for deferred taxation			
(52% × £25 000)		13 000	
Taxation charge:			
ACT on dividends received	3 000		
Corporation tax on profits for year			
(52% × £220 000)	114 400		
		117 400	
			130 400
Net profit after taxation			284 600
Less: Dividend paid		35 000	
Dividend proposed		140 000	
			175 000
Retained profits for the year			109 600

Balance sheet as at 31 December 1982

Fixed assets: Cost		200 000	
Less: Depreciation		40 000	
			160 000
Deferred taxation*			47 000
			207 000
Current assets:			
Stock, debtors and cash		1 469 500	
Less: Current liabilities:			
Trade creditors	264 500		
Proposed dividend	140 000		
ACT on proposed dividend	60 000		
Corporation tax†	102 400		
		566 900	
			902 600
			1 109 600
Share capital:			
Ordinary shares of £1 each			1 000 000
P&L account			109 600
			1 109 600

Notes:

*ACT on proposed dividend $3/7 \times £140\ 000$	=		60 000
Less: Transfer from P&L account re-short-term timing difference			13 000
			47 000
†Tax charge for year, per profit and loss account.			114 400
Less: Balance on ACT account, per trial balance			12 000
			102 400

F A STEP FURTHER   The following references are given for the purpose of further study:

Accounting Digest No. 174 – Deferred Taxation (ICAEW).
VAT General Guide (HM Customs and Excise).
J. Blake, *Accounting Standards* (Longman Professional). Chs 6, 8 and 14.
G. Holmes and A. Sugden, *Interpreting Company Reports and Accounts* (Woodhead-Faulkner). Ch. 13.

Chapter 10

Profit and loss account matters: Extraordinary items and prior year adjustments, and earnings per share

SSAPs 6 and 3

A GETTING STARTED

In this chapter, two standards are discussed: SSAP 6: *Extraordinary Items and Prior Year Adjustments*, and SSAP 3: *Earnings per Share*. Both have a great influence on the way users of the financial information perceive the company's results, and the standardised procedures help to ensure that potential investors and others who may rely on the accounts are not misled.

B ESSENTIAL PRINCIPLES

SSAP 6: *EXTRAORDINARY ITEMS AND PRIOR YEAR ADJUSTMENTS*

The standard defines 'extraordinary items' as follows:

'Extraordinary items are material items which derive from events or transactions that fall outside the ordinary activities of the company and which are therefore expected not to recur frequently or regularly. They do not include exceptional items nor do they include prior year items merely because they relate to a prior year.'

To understand the meaning of 'extraordinary', it is necessary to have a clear understanding of what is meant by 'ordinary', and the standard gives the following definition:

'Ordinary activities are any activities which are usually, frequently or regularly undertaken by the company and any related activities in which the company engages in furtherance of, incidental to, or arising from those activities. They include, but are not confined to, the trading activities of the company.'

Prior year adjustments are defined as:

'. . . those material adjustments applicable to prior years arising from changes in accounting policies or from the correction of fundamental errors. They do not include normal recurring corrections or adjustments of accounting estimates made in prior years.'

The SSAP is based on the view that the P&L account for the year should include not only the current operating profit, but also should show separately all profits and losses including all extraordinary items which are recognised in that year and all prior year items other than prior year adjustments. This is known as the 'all-inclusive' concept of profit, which recognises that the current operating profit alone is not appropriate for all the uses to which the financial statements are put, and that the inclusion and separate disclosure of extraordinary items and prior year adjustments help to give a better view of a company's profitability and progress. In addition, the exclusion of extraordinary items and prior year adjustments could lead to a loss of comparability between the reported results of companies, and also could result in the extraordinary items and prior year adjustments being overlooked in any consideration of results over a series of years.

EXCEPTIONAL ITEMS

The definition of extraordinary items given earlier made reference to 'exceptional items', and these are defined as follows:

'Exceptional items are material items which derive from events or transactions that fall within the ordinary activities of the company, and which need to be disclosed separately by virtue of their size or incidence if the financial statements are to give a true and fair view.'

Examples of exceptional and extraordinary items

The standard gives the following examples:

Exceptional	Extraordinary
(Material items relating to):	(Material profits or losses arising from):
Redundancy costs relating to continuing business segments*	The discontinuance of a business segment,* either through termination or disposal
Reorganisation costs unrelated to the discontinuance of a business segment*	The sale of an investment not acquired with the intention of resale, such as investments in subsidiary and associated companies
Previously capitalised expenditure on intangible fixed assets written off other than as part of a process of amortisation	Provision made for the permanent diminution in value of a fixed asset because of extraordinary events during the period

Exceptional	Extraordinary
Amounts transferred to employee share schemes	The expropriation of assets
Profits or losses on the disposal of fixed assets†	Profits or losses on the disposal of fixed assets†
Abnormal charges for bad debts and write-offs of stock and WIP	Change in the basis of taxation, or a significant change in government fiscal policy
Abnormal provisions for losses on long-term contracts	
Surpluses arising on the settlement of insurance claims	
Amounts received in settlement of insurance claims for consequential loss of profits	

*A business segment is defined as a material and separately identifiable component of the business operations of a company or group whose activities, assets and results can be clearly distinguished from the remainder of the company's activities. A business segment will normally have its own separate product lines or markets.
†The classification of a material surplus or deficit on the disposal of a fixed asset depends upon the nature of the event which gave rise to the disposal.

PROFIT AND LOSS ACCOUNT PRESENTATION

To help put extraordinary items, prior year adjustments and exceptional items into context, an appendix to the standard is reproduced in full below, showing the way in which the various items are disclosed in the consolidated P&L account:

Consolidated Profit and Loss Account

	Note	1986 (£000)	1985 (£000)
Turnover	2	183 000	158 000
Cost of sales		106 140	86 900
Gross profit		76 860	71 100
Distribution costs and admin expenses	3	57 160	52 500
Profit before exceptional item		19 700	18 600
Exceptional item – loss on major contract	4	8 600	—
Profit on ordinary activities before taxation	5	11 100	18 600
Tax on profit on ordinary activities	6	4 500	7 400
Profit on ordinary activities after taxation		6 600	11 200
Minority interests	7	400	370
Profit attributable to members of holding company		6 200	10 830
Extraordinary loss after taxation	8	595	1 020
Profit for the financial year		5 605	9 810
Dividends	9	4 410	4 200
Retained profit for the year	10	1 195	5 610

Movements on reserves are set out in note 10.

(Extracts from Notes)

	1986 (£000)	1985 (£000)
4. Exceptional item		
Exceptional loss on major contract in Middle East	8 600	—
8. Extraordinary loss after taxation		
Extraordinary income:		
Profit on sale of head office	1 030	—
Extraordinary charges:		
Provision for costs of closure of x division	—	1 700
Provision for costs of closure of y division	2 700	—
	2 700	1 700
Extraordinary loss	1 670	1 700
Tax relief on extraordinary loss	670	680
	1 000	1 020
Less: Minority share of provision for closure costs	405	—
Extraordinary loss after tax	595	1 020

10. Movements on reserves

(a) Consolidated

	Profit and loss account	Revaluation reserve
	(£000)	(£000)
At 1 January – as previously reported	48 890	23 400
– prior year adjustment (see below)	450	—
– as restated	48 440	23 400
Retained profit for the year	1 195	—
	49 635	23 400

The prior year adjustment represents the effect of a change in the accounting policy for goodwill. Goodwill, which was previously carried in the balance sheet as a permanent item, is now, as a result of the introduction of SSAP 22 *Accounting for Goodwill*, written off against reserves immediately on acquisition, this being the preferred treatment under that standard. This adjustment has no effect on the reported profit of either the years under review. Goodwill of £450 000 previously carried in the balance sheet has therefore been written off against retained profits at the beginning of 1985.

SUMMARY OF DISCLOSURE REQUIREMENTS

Exceptional items

These are required to be shown as part of profit or loss on ordinary activities, but require separate disclosure due to exceptional size or incidence, usually by way of note. The standard requires the profit before exceptional items and the exceptional items themselves to be disclosed separately in the P&L account where it is necessary in order to give a true and fair view.

Extraordinary items

These are required to be shown in the P&L account, following the ordinary results, but before the deduction of any appropriations such as dividends, and after the figure for minority interests in the case of consolidated accounts.

Where a single extraordinary event gives rise to separate items of income and expenditure, the items are aggregated, with the net balance being included in either extraordinary income or extraordinary charges as appropriate. The amount of each extraordinary item should be shown individually either on the face of the P&L account or in the notes to the accounts. Note that the minority share of extraordinary profit or loss must be shown separately.

Taxation relating to extraordinary items	This must be shown separately, and the standard prescribes a method whereby the overall tax charge is split between that relating to ordinary activities and that relating to extraordinary items. This is achieved by computing the tax charge with and without the extraordinary profit or loss, and attributing the difference to the extraordinary items. By this means, the calculation of earnings per share (see SSAP 3 later in this chapter) is not distorted due to the incidence of the extraordinary items.
Profits/losses from terminated activities	If arising from terminated activities before the commencement of implementation of the closure programme, these are not treated as extraordinary as they are deemed part of the trading results of the year. They may, however, require separate disclosure to enable the results of the *continuing* operations to be ascertained.
Prior year items	The majority of corrections and adjustments relating to prior years are dealt with in the P&L account of the year in which they are identified, and their effect stated where material. Only in the rare cases where prior year adjustments arise from changes in accounting policies and the correction of fundamental errors should an adjustment be made against the opening balance of retained profits or reserves (e.g. the change in the accounting treatment of goodwill in the example P&L account shown earlier). Where accounting policies change, the amounts for the current *and corresponding* periods are restated on the basis of the new policies. Where financial statements include a historical summary (e.g. to comply with Stock Exchange requirements), amounts in the summary should be restated to reflect the changes, with a note appended showing which years have been changed. If this is impractical, a note stating that the summary has not been changed should be given.
Movements on reserves	The standard requires all reserve movements including the movement on retained P&L account, to be disclosed in a single statement of movements on reserves. Reference should be made on the face of the P&L account for the year as to where the statement can be found if it does not immediately follow the P&L account.

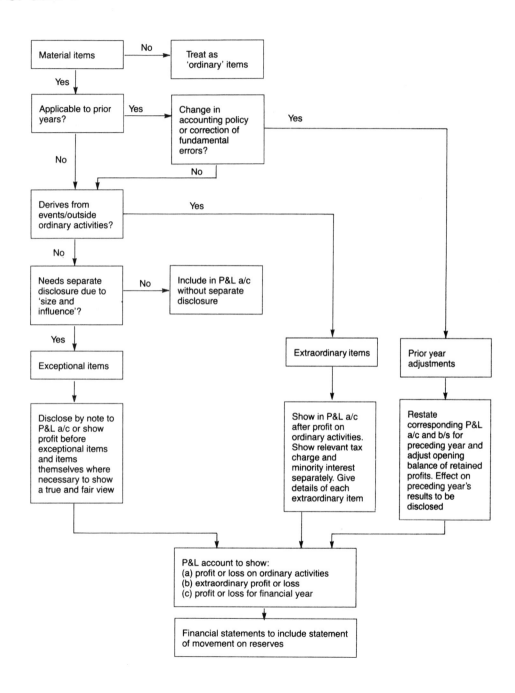

SSAP 3: *EARNINGS PER SHARE*

This standard applies only to *listed* companies, i.e. those whose shares are quoted on a recognised Stock Exchange. The earnings per share (eps) is widely used by investors as an indicator of a company's performance, and the *price–earnings (p/e) ratio*, shown in the *Financial Times* and the financial pages of certain other newspapers is perhaps the clearest indication of the Stock Market's rating of any particular company. The p/e ratio is simply the market price divided by the eps.

Whilst 'market price' is derived from the forces of supply and demand which exist in the stock markets, eps is, as the name implies, the proportion of a company's earnings which is attributable to each equity share, as based on the company's most recently reported profits. For the p/e ratio to have meaning, the eps must be reliable, and consistently calculated both between one company and another, and between one financial period and another. In theory, the eps calculation is based on the following simple formula, as stated in the definition of eps contained within the standard:

'The profit in pence attributable to each equity share, based on the consolidated profit* of the period after tax and after deducting minority interests and preference dividends, but before taking into account extraordinary items, divided by the number of equity shares in issue and ranking for dividend in respect of the period.'

*Including earnings of associated companies.

Or, simply,

$$\frac{\text{Consolidated profit on ordinary activities after tax,}}{\text{No. of equity shares in issue and ranking for dividend}}$$

In practice, however, the calculation is more complicated due to three factors:

(a) taxation complications;
(b) changes in share capital;
(c) future dilution of earnings.

(A) TAXATION COMPLICATIONS

The standards relating to taxation were covered in Chapter 9. When calculating 'after tax' earnings for the purpose of the eps formula it should be recognised that the tax charge may vary depending upon whether the company has any *unrelieved* Advance Corporation Tax (ACT) or unrelieved overseas tax. If it has, then the overall tax charge increases as a result of the payment of dividends, as the ACT linked to the dividends is not able to be offset in full in the usual way against the corporation tax liability.

The standard classifies a company's tax charge between that which is *constant* (i.e. not varying with the proportion of profit distributed by way of dividend) and that which is *variable* according to the amount of profit distributed, and which would be absent if no distributions were made. These components of the tax charge are listed as follows:

Constant	Variable
Corporation tax charge on income	Irrecoverable ACT
Tax attributable to dividends received	Overseas tax unrelieved because dividend payments restrict the double tax credit available
Overseas tax unrelieved because the rate of overseas tax exceeds the rate of UK corporation tax	

Two alternative methods of calculating eps are explained in the standard:

1. 'Net' basis: taking account of both constant and variable tax charge (i.e. profits figure used is 'net of all taxation').
2. 'Nil' basis: taking account only of constant tax charge (i.e. profits figure used is after the tax occurring if distributions were 'nil').

For most companies, the two bases will produce an identical eps figure, but divergent figures will result for certain companies, notably those which have income subject to overseas tax, a significant part of which is distributed.

The advantages claimed for each basis are:

NET basis: takes account of the total tax charge for the period including that arising solely as a result of the dividend policy pursued by the company's directors.

NIL basis: eps figure is not dependent on the level of distribution, thereby making inter-company comparisons more reliable.

The standard favours the **NET** basis on the grounds that it takes into account all relevant facts, whereas the nil basis 'turns a blind eye' to the *variable* tax charge.

If, however, there is a material difference between eps figures when calculated under the two methods, both figures should be disclosed. For an illustration of this in the P&L account of an actual company, see Section C: Useful Aplied Materials.

(B) CHANGES IN SHARE CAPITAL

The formula contained within the definition of eps uses as divisor the number of equity shares in issue and ranking for dividend in respect of the period. Problems arise due to the following events which may take place between the start and end of the accounting period:

1. An issue at full market price;
2. Capitalisation (bonus/scrip) issue and share splits;
3. A share exchange;
4. A rights issue at less than full market price.

In each of the above cases, the formula used for determining eps must be amended, as follows:

1. *Issue at full market price*, i.e. where new equity shares have been issued either for cash at full market price or as consideration for the acquisition of an asset. The eps formula:

$$\frac{\text{Consolidated profit on ordinary activities after tax,}}{\text{Average number of shares ranking for dividend,}}$$
minority interests and preference dividends

Average number of shares ranking for dividend, weighted on a time basis

2. *Capitalisation issue and share splits*, i.e. where reserves have been converted into equity capital by means of a bonus issue, or where equity shares are split into shares of a smaller nominal value. The eps formula:

Consolidated profit on ordinary activities after tax, minority interests and preference dividends

Number of shares ranking for dividend after the capitalisation or split

(The corresponding eps figure for previous periods should be adjusted by using the divisor in the above formula.)

3. *Share exchange*, i.e. where shares have been issued in exchange for shares in a new subsidiary. The eps formula:

Consolidated profit on ordinary activities after tax, minority interests and preference dividends

Average number of shares ranking for dividend, weighted on a time basis*

*Taking the date of issue of the shares as the first day of the period for which the subsidiary's earnings are included in group earnings.

4. *Rights issue at less than full market price*, i.e. where existing shareholders have been invited to buy shares at a discount to the 'pre-rights' market price. It is equivalent to an issue of shares at full market price together with a bonus issue. Because of this bonus element, the eps for previous years must be adjusted for the purpose of comparisons, and the following factor is applied:

Theoretical ex-rights price

Actual cum-rights price

To avoid splitting the eps figure for the current year between that relating to the period before the rights issue and that relating to the period after the rights issue, the share capital prior to the issue is adjusted by the reciprocal of the factor applied to previous years' eps figures, as follows:

$$\frac{\text{Actual cum-rights price}}{\text{Theoretical ex-rights price}}$$

The *theoretical ex-rights price* is the price per ordinary share immediately after the rights issue, as adjusted for the extent to which the rights issue has been offered to shareholders at a discount to the market value.

The *actual cum-rights price* is the price per ordinary share immediately before the rights issue.

Readers are referred to Section D: Recent Examination Questions for worked examples of these calculations.

(C) FUTURE DILUTION OF EARNINGS

If a company has outstanding a separate class of equity shares which do not rank for dividend in the current period but will do so in the future, or has certain types of convertible loan stocks, options or warrants which carry the right for holders to convert into equity shares at some future date, then the effect of these may be to *dilute* the eps in the future.

In each of these cases (unless the dilution is immaterial), in addition to the basic eps, the *fully diluted* eps figure should be shown on the face of the P&L account, together with full information as to the rights of the holders of the stock, warrants, etc. and the basis of the calculation of the diluted eps figure.

The calculation of the eps should be based on the assumption that the maximum number of new equity shares was issued under the terms of the conversion on the first day of the current accounting period. The earnings figure used in the numerator of the formula is increased by the amount of interest (net of tax) on convertible loan stock which would be saved if the conversion rights are exercised by stockholders.

C USEFUL APPLIED MATERIALS

The following extracts (Figs 10.1 and 10.2) are taken from the published accounts of Glynwed International plc, and show the treatment of earnings per share, extraordinary items and a prior year adjustment to reserves, due to a change in accounting policy.

Consolidated Profit and Loss Account

For the 52 weeks ended 28th December 1985	Notes	1985 £million	1984 £million
Turnover	3	**464·1**	514·1
Net ordinary operating costs	4	**(424·5)**	(478·5)
Operating profit	3	**39·6**	35·6
Interest payable (net)	7	**(4·0)**	(9·1)
Profit on ordinary activities before taxation		**35·6**	26·5
Tax on profit on ordinary activities	8	**(12·3)**	(8·2)
Profit on ordinary activities after taxation		**23·3**	18·3
Minority interests		**—**	0·6
Profit after taxation and minority interests		**23·3**	18·9
Preference dividends	9	**(0·1)**	(0·1)
Earnings for the period		**23·2**	18·8
Ordinary dividends	9	**(8·8)**	(7·7)
Extraordinary items	11	**(2·3)**	(3·9)
Profit retained	12 & 25	**12·1**	7·2
Earnings per share — net basis	13	**27·69p**	22·45p
— nil distribution basis		**24·41p**	17·91p

Figure 10.2 Glynwed International plc; notes on the accounts

Notes on the Accounts

11 Extraordinary items

	1985 £million	1984 £million
Losses on disposals and termination costs of discontinued businesses	3·5	2·4
Taxation applicable	(1·2)	1·5
Total extraordinary items	2·3	3·9

13 Calculations of earnings per share

The calculations of earnings per ordinary share are based on the figures set out below and an average of 83·7 million ordinary shares of 25p each (1984 83·7 million) in issue.

	1985 £million	1984 £million
Profit after taxation	23·3	18·3
Minority interests	—	0·6
Preference dividends	(0·1)	(0·1)
Net basis	23·2	18·8
Advance corporation tax recoverable	(2·7)	(3·8)
Nil distribution basis	20·5	15·0
Earnings per share — net basis	27·69p	22·45p
— nil distribution basis	24·41p	17·91p

25 Reserves

	Share premium £million	Revaluation reserve £million	Other reserves £million	Profit and loss account £million	**Total £million**
Group					
Balances at 30th December 1984	21·4	13·2	—	60·3	**94·9**
Change in accounting policy — finance leases	—	—	—	0·2	**0·2**
As restated	21·4	13·2	—	60·5	**95·1**
Exchange differences	—	(0·2)	—	(3·3)	**(3·5)**
Goodwill written off	—	—	—	(0·8)	**(0·8)**
Movement on reserves	—	(0·2)	—	0·2	**—**
Deficit on revaluation of properties	—	(5·9)	—	—	**(5·9)**
Profit retained	—	—	—	12·1	**12·1**
Balances at 28th December 1985	21·4	6·9	—	68·7	**97·0**
Glynwed International plc					
Balances at 30th December 1984	21·4	—	0·8	45·4	**67·6**
Exchange differences	—	—	—	(2·5)	**(2·5)**
Goodwill written off	—	—	—	(0·4)	**(0·4)**
Profit retained	—	—	—	27·6	**27·6**
Balances at 28th December 1985	21·4	—	0·8	70·1	**92·3**

In accordance with SSAP 20, exchange gains of £4·0 million (1984 £6·4 million losses) arising from the translation of foreign currency borrowings used to finance foreign currency investments, have been offset as reserve movements against exchange differences arising on the retranslation of the net investments.

1

(a) SSAP 6 *Extraordinary Items and Prior Year Adjustments* is based on the 'all-inclusive' concept of income rather than the 'current operating' income concept.

Required:

Discuss the merits of BOTH the 'all-inclusive' income and the 'current operating' income concepts.

(*Note*: the current operating income approach is sometimes referred to as reserve accounting.) (8 marks)

(b) State, giving your reasons, whether you consider the following items to be extraordinary, as defined in SSAP 6, and comment upon any additional information that may be necessary for a considered opinion on disclosure.

    (i) An additional £1 million contribution paid by the company to the employees' pension fund. (4 marks)

    (ii) Previously capitalised development expenditure written off. (4 marks)

    (iii) Damages for libel paid by the publishers of a satirical magazine. (4 marks)

(20 marks)

(Chartered Association of Certified Accountants, June 1985)

2 Answer the following questions in accordance with SSAP 3 *Earnings per Share* (eps).

(a) Why is it considered important to measure eps and what figure for earnings should you use when calculating eps for a group of companies with ordinary and preference shares? (8 marks)

(b) Explain the difference between the nil distribution basis and the net basis for calculating eps and give the advantage of each method. (7 marks)

(c) How should you deal with the following situations when calculating eps?

    (i) the issue of a separate class of equity shares which do not rank for any dividend in the period under review, but which will do so in the future. (2 marks)

    (ii) a scrip (or bonus) issue of shares during the year. (2 marks)

    (iii) shares issued during the period as consideration for shares in a new subsidiary. (2 marks)

(d) On 1 January 1983 a company had 3 million ordinary shares of £1 each in issue. On 1 July 1983 the company made a rights issue of 1 for 2 at a price of £1.50. The market price of the existing shares immediately before the rights issue was £2.00. The earnings of the company for the year ended 31 December 1983 were £750 000.

Calculate the EPS for the year ended 31 December 1983.

(4 marks)

(25 marks)

(Chartered Association of Certified Accountants, Dec. 1984)

3 You are given the following information relating to S plc:

Summarised profit and loss account for the year ended 31 December 1985:

	£000	£000
Profit on ordinary activities before taxation		4 131
UK tax on profit on ordinary activities		1 629
Profit on ordinary activities after taxation		2 502
Extraordinary items less taxation		252
		2 250
Minority interest		90
		2 160
Retained profits at 1 January 1985		5 268
		7 428
Dividends:		
Preference	45	
Ordinary	669	
		714
Retained profits at 31 December 1985		6 714

(i) From 1 January 1984 until 31 March 1985 the share capital of S plc consisted of 12 000 000 ordinary shares of 25 pence each (authorised, issued and fully paid) and 900 000 preference shares of £1 each (authorised, issued and fully paid).

(ii) On 1 April 1985 S plc made a 1-for-4 rights issue of ordinary shares at £1.00. The market price of an ordinary share of S plc on the last day of quotation cum rights was £1.50.

(iii) The earnings per share for the year ended 31 December 1984 had been calculated at 15.0 pence.

In accordance with the requirements of Statement of Standard Accounting Practice No. 3, **you are required to:**

(a) calculate the earnings per share of S plc for the year ended 31 December 1985;

(b) calculate the adjusted earnings per share of S plc for the year ended 31 December 1984;

(c) show how the results of your calculations, together with any necessary notes, would be disclosed in the financial statements of S plc. (15 marks)

(Institute of Cost and Management Accountants – Stage 3 Specimen paper, 1986)

1(a) The 'all-inclusive' and 'current operating' income concepts are alternative ways of defining the scope of a company's P&L account. The 'all-inclusive' concept, favoured by SSAP 6, adopts the approach of including all income and expenditure, with separate disclosure within the P&L account of exceptional and extraordinary items where material. Prior year adjustments are disclosed by restating the corresponding P&L account and balance sheet for the preceding year, and adjusting the opening balance of retained profits.

Advantages claimed for this concept are:

- Profit figures are less capable of manipulation since all income and expenditure is included, the contents of the profit and loss account not being subject to the discretion of the preparer.
- As all relevant details are contained within the one statement, the users of the accounts have all the information in an accessible form.

The 'current operating' income concept adopts the approach that the P&L account should reflect only the transactions arising from 'ordinary activities' during the current year, with all other items being taken direct to reserves.

Advantages claimed for this concept are:

- Users may consider the current operating income to be the most important indicator of operating efficiency and future income, and the best figure to be used for inter-company comparisons.
- The less sophisticated user may be confused by the appearance of more than one profit figure, i.e. before and after extraordinary items.

1(b) SSAP 6 defines extraordinary items as material items which derive from events or transactions that fall outside the ordinary activities of the company and which are therefore expected not to recur frequently or regularly. They do not include exceptional items nor do they include prior year items merely because they relate to a prior year.

This definition can be applied to the three items in the question, as follows:

(i) Payments into a pension fund are part of a company's ordinary activities, but the fact that this is an additional contribution of an (apparently) material amount may result in it being treated as *exceptional*, in which case it would be the subject of a note to the P&L account, or disclosed separately within the P&L account if necessary to show a true and fair view.

(ii) The standard states that previously capitalised expenditure which is now written off should be treated as exceptional, and not extraordinary.

(iii) One would assume that part of the ordinary activities of a satirical magazine is to publish *potentially* libellous articles, and therefore when damages are awarded against the publishers, it should not be treated as extraordinary. The amount may, however, be exceptional due to its size and influence, thereby requiring separate disclosure.

2(a) Earnings per share (eps) is widely used by investors as an indicator of a company's performance, being more reliable than measures such as dividend yield. By relating earnings to shares in issue and ranking for dividend, the user of the information can assess the impact on earnings of company expansion where shares have been issued in exchange for acquiring new businesses.

In the case of a group of companies with both ordinary and preference shares, the earnings figure to be used is the consolidated profit on ordinary activities after tax, minority interests and preference dividends, but before extraordinary items.

2(b) The tax charge of a company may have two elements, a constant element which will not vary with the amount of the company's dividends, and a variable element that will change with the amount of the dividend.

Two alternative methods of calculating earnings per share are explained in the standard, the 'net' basis, which takes account of both constant and variable elements of the tax charge, and the 'nil' basis, which takes account only of the constant tax charge.

For most companies, the two bases will produce an identical eps figure, but divergent figures will result for certain companies, notably those which have income subject to overseas tax, a significant part of which is distributed.

The main advantages claimed for each basis are:

Net basis: takes account of the total tax charge for the period including that arising solely as a result of the dividend policy pursued by the company's directors.

Nil basis: eps figure is not dependent on the level of distribution, thereby making inter-company comparisons more reliable.

2(c)
(i) The company should disclose two figures for eps, the basic figure and the fully diluted figure, where the difference between the two is material.

(ii) The eps will be calculated by the earnings being apportioned over the number of shares ranking for dividend after the capitalisation. The corresponding eps figure for previous periods should be adjusted.

(iii) The eps is calculated by the earnings being apportioned over the average number of shares ranking for dividend, weighted on a time basis, taking the date of issue of the shares as the first day of the period for which the subsidiary's earnings are included in group earnings.

2(d)

	£000
Total pre-rights share capital	6 000
Rights issue (1.5 m × £1.50)	2 250
	8 250

Theoretical ex-rights price = £8 250 000 ÷ 4.5 m = £1.83.

Weighted average no. of shares in issue, after applying factor to allow for notional bonus element in rights issue:

6/12 × 3 000 000 × 2.00/1.83	=	1 639 344
6/12 × 4 500 000	=	2 250 000
		3 889 344

$$\frac{\text{Earnings}}{\text{per share}} = \frac{\text{Earnings for year}}{\text{Weighted average no. of shares}} = \frac{£750\,000}{3\,889\,344} = 19.3\text{p}$$

3(a)

	£000	£000
Profit on ordinary activities after taxation		2 502
Less: Minority interest	90	
Preference dividend	45	
		135
Basic earnings		2 367

Theoretical ex-rights price:

12 m shares @ £1.50 = £18 m
3 m shares @ £1.00 = £3 m

£21 m, divided by total shares (15 m) = £1.40

Shares in issue, adjusted for bonus element in rights issue:

$$12\text{ m} \times \frac{1.50}{1.40} \times \frac{3}{12} = 3\,214\,285$$

$$15\text{ m} \times \frac{9}{12} = 11\,250\,000$$

$$14\,464\,285$$

$$\text{Basic earnings per share} = \frac{£2\,367\,000}{14\,464\,285} = 16.4\text{p}$$

3(b)

eps for previous year = 15p

Adjusted by factor: $\dfrac{\text{Theoretical ex-rights price}}{\text{Actual cum-rights price}}$

$$15p \times \frac{1.40}{1.50} = 14p$$

3(c) The basic eps figure (16.4p) will be stated on the face of the P&L account, together with the adjusted eps (14p) for the previous period. The basis of calculation should be disclosed, revealing the amount of the earnings and the number of shares used in the calculation.

F   A STEP FURTHER

The following references are given for the purpose of further study:

Selected Accounting Standards – Interpretation Problems Explained (ICAEW), pp. 159–200.
F. A. J. Couldery, *Accounting Standards Study Book* (Gee). Chs 3 and 6.
R. K. Ashton, *UK Financial Accounting Standards* (Woodhead-Faulkner). Chs 4 and 6.

Chapter 11

Balance sheet matters: Post balance sheet events and contingencies

SSAPs 17 and 18

262

A   GETTING STARTED

According to the 'official terminology' published by the Institute of Cost and Management Accountants, a balance sheet is:

'A statement of the financial position of an entity at a given date disclosing the value of the assets, liabilities and accumulated funds such as shareholders' contributions and reserves, prepared to give a true and fair view of the state of the entity at that date.'

The 'true and fair view' cannot be given solely by listing the relevant balances as appear in the ledger at the 'given date'. Comprehensive notes are appended which not only explain the accounting policies adopted but also give detailed information to ensure compliance with company law, accounting standards and possibly Stock Exchange requirements. This chapter concerns two standards which might be the subject of notes, relating firstly to certain events which occur *after* the balance sheet date and secondly to conditions which, though in existence at the balance sheet date, will be confirmed only on the occurrence (or non-occurrence) of one or more uncertain future events.

B ESSENTIAL PRINCIPLES

SSAP 17: ACCOUNTING FOR POST BALANCE SHEET EVENTS

It may come as a surprise to students that events occurring after the date of the balance sheet need be considered when drawing up the financial statements. In practice, they need to be reflected in the statements only if they are material and provide additional evidence of conditions that existed at the balance sheet date.

The 'post balance sheet period' during which such events might arise starts at the date of the balance sheet and ends with the date on which the financial statements are approved by the board of directors. This is usually the date of the company's (or holding company's, in the case of group accounts) board meeting at which the approval is given. The date is always shown in the statements, usually at the foot of the 'Director's report'.

The standard excludes any *preliminary consideration* given by directors within the post balance sheet period to matters which may lead to decisions being taken at some future date. However, relevant information concerning any material events occurring after the end of the post balance sheet period *should* be published, to avoid misleading the users of the financial statements. An example is given in Section C: Useful Applied Materials.

CLASSIFICATION

The definition of a post balance sheet event is given in the standard as follows:

'. . . those events, both favourable and unfavourable, which occur between the balance sheet date and the date on which the financial statements are approved by the board of directors'.

They are divided between *adjusting* events (i.e. those which require figures to be adjusted within the financial statements) and *non-adjusting* events which, as their name implies, do not require any changes to amounts, but need only be 'noted'.

The distinction between the two depends upon whether they relate to conditions existing at the balance sheet date, as the following example illustrates.

A company has a financial year which ends on 31 March 1987. Before the accounts are approved by the directors, consideration is given to the following matters:

1. A plot of land was sold on 10 March 1987, at a price which was determined by an independent valuation in April 1987.
2. A factory building was acquired in April 1987.

Both are regarded as material events.

The first item is an **adjusting** event, as the valuation provides additional evidence of conditions existing at the balance sheet date. As such, the determined price will be incorporated within the financial statements for the year ended 31 March 1987.

The second item is **non-adjusting**, as it concerns conditions which did not exist at the date of the balance sheet. The accounts will include a note giving details of the acquisition, for the purpose of providing users with additional and relevant information on which to judge the company's performance and prospects.

Adjusting events

In addition to the subsequent determination of the purchase price of assets as illustrated in the previous section, an appendix to the standard gives the following examples of 'adjusting events':

(a) *Fixed assets*. The subsequent determination of the proceeds of sale of assets purchased or sold before the year end.

(b) *Property*. A valuation which provides evidence of a permanent diminution in value.

(c) *Investments*. The receipt of a copy of the financial statements or other information in respect of an unlisted company which provides evidence of a permanent diminution in the value of a long-term investment.

(d) *Stocks and work in progress*.
   (i) The receipt of proceeds of sales after the balance sheet date or other evidence concerning the net realisable value of stocks.
   (ii) The receipt of evidence that the previous estimate of accrued profit on a long-term contract was materially inaccurate.

(e) *Debtors*. The renegotiation of amounts owing by debtors, or the insolvency of a debtor.

(f) *Dividends receivable*. The declaration of dividends by subsidiaries and associated companies relating to periods prior to the balance sheet date of the holding company.

(g) *Taxation*. The receipt of information regarding rates of taxation.

(h) *Claims*. Amounts received or receivable in respect of insurance claims which were in the course of negotiation at the balance sheet date.

(i) *Discoveries*. The discovery of errors or frauds which show that the financial statements were incorrect.

Note that there is usually no necessity to disclose adjusting events as separate items in the financial statements.

Adjusting events and the 'going concern' concept

As stated in SSAP 2 (see Ch. 4), the going concern concept assumes that the enterprise will continue in operational existence for the foreseeable future. It sometimes happens that events occur during the post balance sheet period which give cause for doubt as to the appropriateness of applying the concept when preparing the financial statements. Examples might include the liquidation of a major debtor or the existence of worsening cash flow problems. The standard requires such matters to be treated as adjusting events where they indicate that the application of the going concern concept to the whole or a material part of the company is not appropriate.

Non-adjusting events

In addition to a list of suggested adjusting events, the appendix to the standard provides examples of non-adjusting events, as follows:

(a) mergers and acquisitions;
(b) reconstructions and proposed reconstructions;

(c)   issues of shares and debentures;

(d)   purchases and sales of fixed assets and investments;

(e)   losses of fixed assets or stocks as a result of a catastrophe such as a fire or flood;

(f)   opening new trading activities or extending existing trading activities;

(g)   closing a significant part of the trading activities if this was not anticipated at the year end;

(h)   decline in the value of property and investments held as fixed assets, if it can be demonstrated that the decline occurred after the year end;

(i)   changes in rates of foreign exchange;

(j)   government action, such as nationalisation;

(k)   strikes and other labour disputes;

(l)   augmentation of pension benefits.

In exceptional circumstances, compliance with the prudence concept (see SSAP 2) may require non-adjusting events to be reclassified as adjusting, with full details being given in the financial statements. Additionally, non-adjusting events will require disclosure in circumstances where non-disclosure would affect the ability of those using accounts to have a proper understanding of the company's position.

POST BALANCE SHEET EVENTS AND 'WINDOW DRESSING'

Window dressing has been defined* as:

'Transactions, the purpose of which is to arrange affairs so that the financial statements of the concern give a misleading or unrepresentative impression of its financial position.'

*Technical Release 603, ICAEW, issued December 1985.

Examples of window dressing include circular transactions, where two or more companies enter into transactions, with each other, of equivalent values, the purpose being to inflate amounts stated in the financial statements of one or more of the companies, with the transactions being reversed after the year end.

SSAP 17 requires that such alterations be disclosed where they are material, to avoid misleading the users of the financial statements.

INFORMATION TO BE GIVEN ON DISCLOSURE

As stated previously, those post balance sheet events which are non-adjusting or represent the reversal of 'window dressing' transactions may require disclosure in the financial statements. In such cases, the following information should be given:

(a)   the nature of the event;

(b)   an estimate of the financial effect, or a statement that it is not practicable to make such an estimate.

Relevant extracts from published company accounts are given in Section C: Useful Applied Materials.

SUMMARY OF SSAP 17

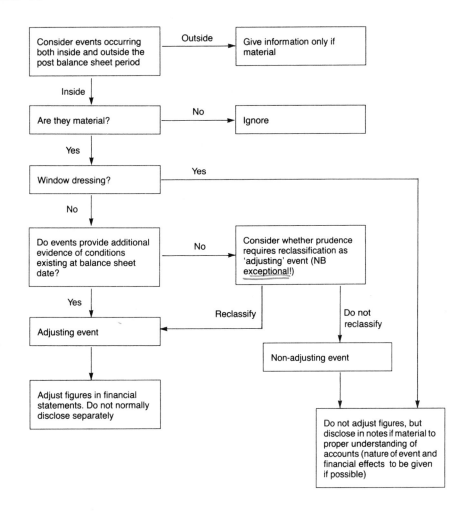

SSAP 18: *ACCOUNTING FOR CONTINGENCIES*

As was seen in the previous section, one of the areas with which SSAP 17 is concerned is that of 'adjusting events', i.e. those events occurring in the post balance sheet period which provide *additional* evidence of conditions that existed at the balance sheet date SSAP 18 is also concerned with conditions existing at the balance sheet date, but only in respect of those where the outcome will be confirmed on the occurrence or non-occurrence of uncertain *future* events. Such conditions are known as *contingencies.* One example of a contingency is a claim for damages, which may or may not cause loss to a company, dependent upon the outcome of a judicial verdict.

The standard does not apply to uncertainties connected with

accounting estimates, such as the anticipated lives of fixed assets or the expected outcome of long-term contracts. Nor does it apply to *remote* contingencies, where disclosure could be misleading.

In the financial statements, contingencies should be taken into consideration as detailed in the headings below.

CONTINGENT LOSSES

A contingent loss (e.g. a claim for damages made against the company) should, if material, be accrued in the financial statements where it is probable that a future event will confirm a loss which can be estimated with reasonable accuracy at the date on which the financial statements are approved by the board of directors. In deciding upon the outcome of the contingency, the directors may rely upon the opinion of experts and advisers, or consider the experience of the company in similar cases in previous years.

If an estimate of the loss is not practicable, the existence of the contingency should be disclosed by way of note, except where the possibility of loss is remote. In circumstances where the risk of loss is *not* remote, but is improbable, the contingency must be noted.

CONTINGENT GAINS

A contingent gain (e.g. a claim for damages made by the company) should not be accrued in the financial statements, and should be disclosed only if it is probable that the gain will be realised.

If the realisation of the gain is *reasonably* certain, it is not a contingency and may be accrued in the financial statements.

For examples of the presentation of both contingent losses and gains, refer to Section C: Useful Applied Materials.

DISCLOSURE REQUIREMENTS

Where disclosure is required, the following information should be given in notes:

(a) the nature of the contingency;
(b) the uncertainties which are expected to affect the ultimate outcome;
(c) a prudent estimate of the potential financial effect (before taking any taxation implications into account), made at the date on which the financial statements are approved by the board of directors; or a statement that it is not practicable to make such an estimate. In the case of a contingent loss, this should be reduced by:
  (i) any amounts accrued;
  (ii) the amounts of any part of the contingency where the possibility of loss is remote.
  (iii) the probable outcome of any counter-claims. Disclosure of such counter-claims should be made where appropriate.
  Only the net amount need be disclosed.
(d) The taxation implications of a contingency crystallising, where appropriate for a full understanding of the financial position.

If the contingency relates to many similar transactions (e.g. guarantees given by a holding company in respect of the overdrafts of its subsidiaries), the separate contingencies need not be individually disclosed, but can be amalgamated.

SUMMARY OF SSAP 18

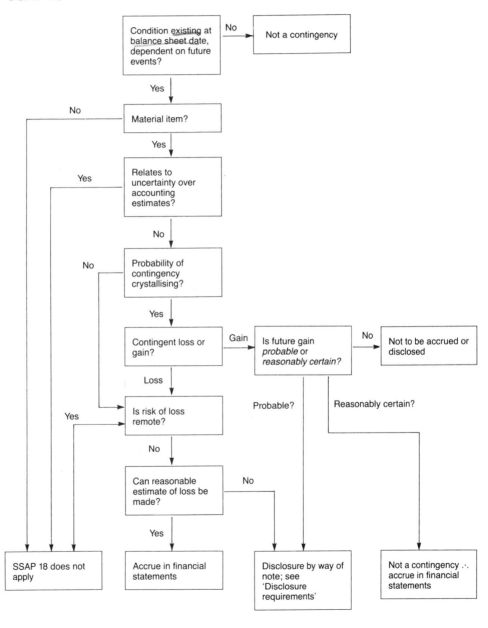

The following (Figs 11.1–11.4) are relevant extracts from the
published accounts of several UK public limited companies.

Figure 11.1 United Biscuits (Holdings) plc; contingent liabilities and
post balance sheet events.

26.   Contingent liabilities

	Group		Company	
	1985 **£m**	1984 £m	**1985** **£m**	1984 £m
Guarantees given under the group's house purchase scheme (including £3,900 in respect of an officer of the company)	**0.2**	0.2	**0.2**	0.2
Guarantees by the company of subsidiaries' borrowings (mainly foreign currency)	—	—	**142.8**	169.2
Contingent liability under VAT group election	—	—	**7.7**	6.9
	0.2	0.2	**150.7**	176.3

27.   Litigation

The Procter & Gamble Company ("P&G"), having obtained a patent in the USA in respect of a soft cookie product, has brought patent infringement and unfair competition claims in the US courts against Keebler Company ("Keebler"), a wholly owned subsidiary of the company, in respect of its "Soft Batch" cookie range. P&G is seeking an injunction against the manufacture and sale by Keebler of this range of products, in addition to monetary damages which have not been quantified. The allegations are being refuted and the action is being strongly defended.
In the opinion of the directors this will not have a significant effect on the group's financial position. Similar claims have been brought by P&G against the two other major soft cookie manufacturers, Nabisco Brands Inc. and Frito-Lay, Inc.

29.   Post balance sheet event

Since the end of the financial year the company made an offer to acquire the whole of the share capital of Imperial Group public limited company ("Imperial"). This offer lapsed on 11th April 1986.

On 17th and 18th February 1986, Morgan Grenfell & Co. Limited ("Morgan Grenfell") purchased in aggregate 113 million ordinary shares in Imperial, representing 14.94 per cent of the issued share capital of Imperial. Subsequently, Morgan Grenfell sold these shares to Morgan Grenfell Investments Limited who on 10th April 1986 sold them to an associate of the company at an aggregate cost of £372.9m. This investment has been financed by £370m of borrowings of the associate secured on the shares purchased and guaranteed by the company and £2.9m of subordinated loan notes of the associate issued to the company.

Figure 11.2 Grand Metropolitan plc; contingent liabilities

24 Contingent Liabilities

The company has guaranteed certain borrowings of subsidiary companies, related companies and third parties. At 30th September, 1985 these amounted to £617m, £3m and £102m respectively (1984—£644m, £2m and £92m respectively). The group has guaranteed borrowings of related companies and third parties which at 30th September, 1985 amounted to £9m and £159m respectively (1984—£7m and £158m respectively).

In addition, there are a number of legal claims or potential claims against the group, the outcome of which cannot at present be foreseen. Full provision is made in these financial statements for all liabilities which are expected to materialise.

Figure 11.3 Ladbroke Group plc; contingencies

29 Contingencies

(a) Guarantees have been given by the parent company in the ordinary course of business in respect of loans and overdrafts granted to subsidiaries amounting to £309.5m (1984 £211.0m), which are already included in the group balance sheet; rent liabilities of subsidiaries; rent liabilities, related to presently or formerly owned freehold and leasehold properties, of third party tenants; and performance undertakings on contracts entered into by subsidiaries.

(b) Under the terms of the property development management contract for the Barclays Bank headquarters office building in New York, a group company could, in extreme circumstances, be required to assume title to the building. The estimated completed cost is £111m which would be financed by the assignment of the related borrowings. This requirement can only arise if physical completion of the building occurs after October 1986, or after October 1987 if the delay is caused by force majeure. It is anticipated that the building will reach substantial completion by June 1986.

Figure 11.4 Exco International plc; contingency resulting in profit

(10) At 31st December 1984 the group had a commitment in respect of an underwriting agreement which has subsequently been concluded at a profit.

D RECENT EXAMINATION QUESTIONS

1 According to Statement of Standard Accounting Practice No. 17 (SSAP 17) events occurring after the balance sheet date may be classified into two categories: 'adjusting events' and 'non-adjusting events'. A similar position is evident in International Accounting Standard No. 10 (IAS 10).

Similarly according to SSAP 18 the treatment of a contingency existing at the balance sheet date is determined by its expected outcome and again IAS 10 recognises this position.

Post balance sheet events – examples listed in SSAP 17:

(i) Subsequent determination of the purchase price or of the proceeds of sale of assets purchased or sold before the year end.
(ii) Renegotiation of amounts owing by debtors or the insolvency of a debtor.
(iii) Changes in rates of foreign exchange.
(iv) Issue of shares and debentures.
(v) Losses of fixed assets or stocks as a result of a catastrophe such as a fire or flood.

(vi) Amounts received or receivable in respect of insurance claims which were in the course of negotiation at the balance sheet date.

(vii) Receipt of evidence that the previous estimate of accrued profit on a long-term contract was materially inaccurate.

(viii) Opening new trading activities or extending existing trading activities.

(ix) Discovery of errors or frauds which show that the financial statements were incorrect.

(x) Strikes and other labour disputes.

Required:

(a) Explain why it should be considered necessary to draw up statements of standard accounting practice to cover the accounting treatment of post balance sheet events and contingencies. (10 marks)

(b) Say whether each of the post balance sheet events mentioned above is an 'adjusting event' or a 'non-adjusting event', explaining why in each case. (10 marks)

(c) Give two examples of contingencies. (2 marks)

(Total 22 marks)

(Institute of Chartered Secretaries and Administrators, Pilot paper, 1986 Syllabus)

2 'Financial statements should be prepared on the basis of conditions existing at the balance sheet date.' SSAP 17 *Accounting for Post Balance Sheet Events*.

(a) Recognising the possibility of time lags in establishing what conditions actually exist at the balance sheet date, how does SSAP 17 seek to ensure that financial accounts are prepared in accordance with this rule?

(10 marks)

(b) How does SSAP 17 seek to ensure that financial accounts prepared in accordance with this rule are not misleading?

(10 marks)

Your answer should include **THREE** examples relating to (a) and a further **THREE** examples relating to (b). (20 marks)

(Chartered Association of Certified Accountants, Dec. 1983)

E   ANSWERS

1(a) A post balance sheet event is defined in SSAP 17 as follows:

'. . . those events, both favourable and unfavourable, which occur between the balance sheet date and the date on which the financial statements are approved by the board of directors'.

A contingency is defined in SSAP 18 as:

'. . . a condition which exists at the balance sheet date, where the outcome will be confirmed only on the occurrence or non-occurrence of one or more uncertain future events.'

The standards were introduced to ensure that financial statements show a true and fair view based not only on the amounts appearing within a company's bookkeeping system, but also when viewed in a wider context. Post balance sheet events can be either 'adjusting' or 'non-adjusting'; the former relate to conditions which exist at the balance sheet date, and require adjustments to be made to amounts contained within the financial statements. 'Non-adjusting' events concern conditions which did not exist at the balance sheet date, but require a note to be made, to provide additional information to help the users gain a fuller understanding of the company's trading environment. This theme of increasing the amount of relevant information contained within the financial statements is repeated in SSAP 18, which states that contingent losses should be accrued where it is probable that they will be confirmed by a future event and the amount can be estimated with reasonable accuracy, or disclosed by way of note if such an estimate is impracticable, except where the possibility of loss is remote. Contingent gains should not be accrued, but should be disclosed only if it is probable that the gain will be realised.

1(b) *Adjusting events*: items (i), (ii), (vi), (vii), (ix). All these items refer to conditions which exist at the balance sheet date, and therefore require adjustments to be made to the relevant amounts appearing in the financial statements.

Non-adjusting events: items (iii), (iv), (v), (viii), (x). These items refer to conditions which did not exist at the balance sheet date, and therefore do not require any changes to be made to amounts appearing in the financial statements. They should be the subject of a note to the accounts.

1(c) Two examples of contingencies:

- A claim for damages made against the company;
- Guarantees given by a holding company to a bank in respect of loans and overdrafts granted to subsidiaries.

2(a) The accrual concept is applied as part of normal accounting procedures in respect of certain transactions which begin prior to the year end but are not completed until after the year end. SSAP 17 refers to events in the post balance sheet period, i.e. from the balance sheet date to the date on which the financial statements are approved by the board of directors. Such post balance sheet events are divided into 'adjusting' and 'non-adjusting' events. If the events provide additional evidence about the conditions existing at the balance sheet date, the financial statements must be adjusted to reflect this information. Examples of adjusting events are:

1. The receipt of proceeds of sales after the balance sheet date or other evidence concerning the net realisable value of stocks.
2. The receipt of information regarding rates of taxation.
3. The discovery of errors or frauds which show that the financial statements were incorrect.

2(b) Whilst adjusting events are those post balance sheet events which provide additional evidence about the conditions existing at the balance sheet date, and require adjustments to be made to the financial statements, there is a second category of post balance sheet event, 'non-adjusting', which, as its name implies, does not result in changes being made to the financial statements, but requires the information to be shown by way of note.

Examples of non-adjusting events are:

1. Issues of shares and debentures;
2. Strikes and other labour disputes;
3. Opening new trading activities or extending existing trading activities.

As can be seen from these examples, they relate to information about the company's business in the post balance sheet period which may affect the user's understanding of the state of the company. None of the examples refer to conditions existing at the balance sheet date, and it is not the intention of SSAP 17 that the accounts should be held open indefinitely to include all events pertinent to the company's affairs. The 'time intervals' concept (see Ch. 4) tells us that financial statements are prepared for a period of time and events occur either in one period or another. The classification of certain post balance sheet events as 'non-adjusting' overcomes the problem by allowing the financial statements to carry additional information about the current circumstances of the company, without the financial statements being affected.

F   A STEP FURTHER

The following reference is given for the purpose of further study:

Selected Accounting Standards – Interpretation Problems Explained (ICAEW), pp. 27–54, 77–94.

Chapter 12

Associated companies, groups of companies and accounting for acquisitions and mergers

SSAPs 1, 14 and 23

A GETTING STARTED	This textbook is published by a company called Longman Group UK Limited, which is a *subsidiary* company of Pearson plc. In the published annual report of Pearson plc for the year ended 31 December 1985, that company listed twelve subsidiaries, including Longman, and in addition, set out the names of eleven partnerships and *associated* companies in which significant interests were held.

In this chapter, we look at the standards relating to groups of companies and associated companies, and also the standard which refers to the ways in which companies which merge with another company can be accounted for. |
| **B   ESSENTIAL PRINCIPLES**

SSAP 1: *ACCOUNTING FOR ASSOCIATED COMPANIES* | The first SSAP to be issued, it was introduced to give a standard accounting treatment for investments in companies which, whilst not being subsidiaries, are subject to significant influence by the investing company.

It is accepted accounting practice that the P&L account of an individual company should only be credited with declared dividends from its investments, and should not be credited with its share of the profits and losses of the companies in which the investments have been made. This is in accordance with the fundamental concept of prudence in not taking credit for investment income until it is received or receivable. Whilst this practice is still applicable for individual |

companies, the view is taken that if a company conducts an important part of its business through the medium of other companies, the mere disclosure of dividend income from these companies is insufficient to give adequate information to the users of the financial statements regarding the way in which the business is operating.

Accordingly, SSAP 1 was introduced to extend the coverage of *consolidated* financial statements to include the share of earnings or losses of *associated companies*. Specifically, the investing company's share of associated companies' profits and losses would be reflected in its consolidated P&L account, and its share of their post-acquisition retained profits and accumulated deficits would be reflected in its consolidated balance sheet, though not in its own balance sheet. This is usually referred to as the *equity method of accounting*, the full definition of which is given later in the chapter (see SSAP 14: *Group Accounts*).

The standard contains the following definition of an associated company:

'An associated company is defined as a company, not being a subsidiary of the investing group or company in which:

(a) the interest of the investing group or company is effectively that of a partner in a joint venture or consortium and the investing group or company is in a position to exercise a significant influence over the company in which the investment is made; or

(b) the interest of the investing group or company is for the long term and is substantial and, having regard to the disposition of the other shareholdings, the investing group or company is in a position to exercise a significant influence over the company in which the investment is made.'

(The accounting treatment of subsidiaries is dealt with in SSAP 14, later in the chapter.)

The standard gives detailed guidance regarding the decision as to whether the investing group or company exercises a *significant influence* over the company in which the investment is made, and the following is a summary of the relevant sections:

Circumstance	Significant influence?
Participation in financial and operating policy decisions (including dividend policy)	Yes, but control of such policies not needed
Representation on board of directors.	Possibly, but not conclusive evidence
Over 20% of equity voting rights owned, where interest is not that of a partner or joint venturer	Yes, unless it can be clearly demonstrated otherwise (e.g. by existence of other major shareholders)
Less than 20% of equity voting rights owned, where interest is not that of a partner or joint venturer	No, unless it can be clearly demonstrated otherwise

ACCOUNTING TREATMENT

Adjustments similar to those adopted for the purpose of presenting consolidated financial statements (see SSAP 14) should be made to exclude from the investing group's financial statements such items as unrealised profits on stocks transferred to and from associated companies.

The names of the principal associated companies should be disclosed in the financial statements of the investing group, together with details of the proportion of the share capital owned, and an indication of the nature of their business. The main requirements of the standard regarding the accounting treatment of associated companies are as follows.

A Investing company's own financial statements:

- Dividends received and receivable are shown in the P&L account. In the balance sheet, the investing company's interests in the associated companies should be shown at cost less any amounts written off.

B Investing group's consolidated financial statements:

- The investing group's share of profits less losses of associated companies are shown, with the breakdown as shown under the following headings.

Consolidated Profit and loss account

- Share of before-tax profits less losses of associated companies, suitably described.
- The tax attributable to the share of profits of associated companies disclosed separately within the group tax charge.
- *Extraordinary items*: if extraordinary items of the associated company would be regarded as extraordinary in the context of the investing group's results, then the share of such items should be disclosed separately from extraordinary items arising from companies belonging to the group.
- The investing group's share of aggregate net profits less losses retained by associated companies.
- Other items, such as the turnover and total profits less losses before tax of the associated companies would only be disclosed (by way of note) if they were so material in the context of the investing group that more detailed information would assist in giving a true and fair view.

If an investing company has an associated company or companies, but not subsidiaries, then it will not prepare a consolidated P&L account, but should show the information required by preparing a separate P&L account or by providing supplementary information to its own P&L account.

Consolidated Balance sheet

The following information relating to associated companies is to be given in the consolidated balance sheet:

- The investing group's interests in associated companies, i.e. the total of:
    - (i) the investing group's share of the net assets other than goodwill (using a 'fair value' basis);

(ii) the investing group's share of any goodwill in the associated company's own financial statements;

(iii) the premium paid (or discount) on the acquisition of the interests in the associated companies in so far as it has not already been written off or amortised.

- Loans to and from associated companies should be disclosed separately.

- Trading balances arising from unsettled normal trading transactions need only be disclosed separately if material in the context of the financial statements of the investing group.

- More detailed information concerning the associated company's assets and liabilities should be disclosed (by way of note) if it is so material in the context of the financial statements of the investing group that the additional information would assist in giving a true and fair view.

- The investing group's share of the post-acquisition accumulated reserves of associated companies and any movements therein should be disclosed.

Section C: Useful Applied Materials includes extracts from the 1986 Annual report of J. Sainsbury plc, showing *inter alia*, the way in which that company discloses details concerning its associated companies.

SSAP 14: *GROUP ACCOUNTS*

Consolidated financial statements are one form of group accounts which presents the information contained in the separate financial statements of a holding company and its subsidiaries as if they were the financial statements of a single entity.

The standard on group accounts does not concern itself with the technicalities of how consolidated accounts are produced, but instead concentrates on the circumstances under which they should be prepared. Readers who wish to familiarise themselves with the techniques of consolidations should refer to Section F: A Step Further.

The definition of a subsidiary company given in the standard is as follows:

'A company shall be deemed to be a subsidiary of another if but only if,

(a) that other either:
    (i) is a member of it and controls the composition of its board of directors; or
    (ii) holds more than half in nominal value of its equity share capital; or
(b) the first mentioned company is a subsidiary of any company which is that other's subsidiary,

and it otherwise comes within the terms of (Section 736 of) the Companies Act (1985).'

The standard confirms the view that consolidated financial statements are usually the best means of achieving the objective of group accounts, which is to give a true and fair view of the P&L and of the state of affairs of the group, and alternative forms of group accounts should only be used in exceptional circumstances.

In giving a true and fair view of the group's results, the same principles apply to consolidated financial statements as would apply to the financial statements of a single entity, and the same disclosure requirements are applicable.

The requirements of the standard are dealt with under the following major headings:

(a) consolidated financial statements;
(b) uniform accounting policies;
(c) group accounting periods and dates;
(d) exclusion of subsidiaries from group accounts and consolidation;
(e) accounting treatment of subsidiaries excluded from consolidation;
(f) disclosure in respect of subsidiaries excluded from consolidation;
(g) changes in composition of the group;
(h) effective date of acquisition or disposal;
(i) disclosure of principal subsidiaries;
(j) outside or minority interests;
(k) restrictions on distributions.

CONSOLIDATED FINANCIAL STATEMENTS

A holding company should prepare group accounts in the form of a single set of consolidated financial statements covering the holding company and its subsidiary companies, subject to certain exceptions (see 'Exclusion of subsidiaries from group accounts and consolidation' below). The accounting bases for consolidation should be disclosed. (See Section C: Useful Applied Materials for the relevant extract from the annual report of J. Sainsbury plc.)

UNIFORM ACCOUNTING POLICIES

Uniform group accounting policies should be followed by a holding company in preparing its consolidated financial statements, making appropriate adjustments to the financial statements of subsidiaries where appropriate. Exceptionally, where such conformity is impractical, different accounting treatments may be used, provided that they are generally acceptable, and disclosure is made of:

● the different accounting policies used;
● an indication of the amounts of the assets and liabilities involved, and where practicable, an indication of the effect on results and net assets of the adoption of policies different from those of the group;
● the reasons for the different treatment.

GROUP ACCOUNTING PERIODS AND DATES

Wherever practicable, all subsidiaries should prepare their financial statements to the same accounting date and for identical accounting periods as the holding company. In certain circumstances, this may cause difficulties; for example, a group with a year end of 30

November might have a subsidiary which operates a retail store. For that subsidiary, a year end away from the peak pre-Christmas selling period would be desirable.

Adjustments should be made to the consolidated financial statements for any abnormal transactions occurring between the group's year end and those of the subsidiaries with differing year ends. In addition, for any subsidiary whose financial period is not coterminous with that of its holding company, disclosure should be made of its name, accounting date, and the reason for using a different accounting date.

EXCLUSION OF SUBSIDIARIES FROM GROUP ACCOUNTS AND CONSOLIDATION, AND ACCOUNTING TREATMENT OF SUBSIDIARIES EXCLUDED FROM CONSOLIDATION

The standard sets out various circumstances whereby certain companies may be excluded from group accounts and consolidation, together with the accounting treatment to be adopted in such cases. The following is a summary of the relevant sections:

Circumstances	Exemptions allowed	Accounting treatment
Holding company is itself a wholly owned subsidiary at its year end	Group accounts need not be prepared for a 'group within a group'	Not applicable
Subsidiary's activities are so dissimilar from other group companies that consolidated financial statements would be misleading	Exclude from consolidation if separate financial statements would provide better information for shareholders and other users	Separate financial statements to be included with group accounts, disclosing a note of the holding company's interest, details of intra-group balances, the nature of transactions with the rest of the group, and a reconciliation with the amount shown as 'investment in subsidiary' in the group accounts, shown under the equity method of accounting*
Holding company, whilst owning over 50% of equity capital of the subsidiary, does not control over 50% of the votes	Exclude subsidiary from consolidation	Equity method of accounting* applies if company satisfies 'associated company' criteria as per SSAP 1, otherwise treat as an investment at cost or valuation, less any provision required
Holding company, whilst owning over 50% of equity capital of the subsidiary, has contractual or other restrictions on its ability to appoint the majority of the board of directors	Exclude subsidiary from consolidation	Equity method of accounting* applies if company satisfies 'associated company' criteria as per SSAP 1, otherwise treat as an investment at cost or valuation, less any provision required

Circumstances	Exemptions allowed	Accounting treatment
Subsidiary operates under severe restrictions which significantly impair control by the holding company over the subsidiary's assets and operations for the foreseeable future (e.g. as a result of political pressure by hostile governments)	Exclude subsidiary from consolidation	Include under equity method of accounting* at the date restrictions came into force. Provide for any permanent losses via consolidated P&L account. Disclosure to be made of subsidiary's net assets and profits or losses for period. Dividends received and amounts written off investment in consolidated P&L account to be shown
Control of subsidiary by holding company is intended to be temporary	Exclude subsidiary from consolidation	State investment in consolidated balance sheet as a current asset at the lower of cost and net realisable value.

Note:
Where subsidiaries have been excluded from consolidation for one or more of the reasons stated, the reasons must be disclosed, and consideration will need to be given as to whether the group's results as a whole give a true and fair view.

* Although the 'equity method' of accounting has been referred to in the earlier part of this chapter in connection with accounting for associated companies, it is perhaps surprising that its definition is contained within SSAP 14 and not SSAP 1 as follows:

'A method of accounting under which the investment in a company is shown in the consolidated balance sheet at:

(a) the cost of the investment; and
(b) the investing company or group's share of the post-acquisition retained profits and reserves of the company; less
(c) any amounts written off in respect of (a) and (b) above;

and under which the investing company accounts separately in its P&L account for its share of the profits before tax, taxation and extraordinary items of the company concerned.'

DISCLOSURE IN RESPECT OF SUBSIDIARIES EXCLUDED FROM CONSOLIDATION

Where subsidiaries are excluded from consolidation, the following information should be disclosed:

(a) the reasons for excluding the subsidiary from the consolidation;
(b) the names of the principal subsidiaries excluded;
(c) any premium or discount on acquisition (in comparison with the fair value of assets acquired) to the extent not written off; and
(d) any further detailed information required by the Companies Act.

CHANGES IN COMPOSITION OF THE GROUP

When a subsidiary is acquired, a computation will be required of the premium or discount on acquisition (i.e. goodwill or capital reserve), on a fair value basis, in accordance with SSAP 22 (see Ch. 6). The consolidated financial statements 'should contain sufficient information about the results of the subsidiaries acquired or sold to enable shareholders to appreciate the effect on the consolidated results'. In particular, when there is a material disposal of a subsidiary, the consolidated P&L account should include:

(a) the subsidiary's results up to the date of disposal; and
(b) the gain or loss on the sale of the investment, being the difference at the time of sale between:
   (i) the proceeds of the sale; and
   (ii) the holding company's share of its net assets together with any premium (less any amounts written off) or discount on acquisition.

EFFECTIVE DATE OF ACQUISITION OR DISPOSAL

The effective date of acquisition or disposal of a subsidiary should be the earlier of:

(a) the date on which the consideration passes; or
(b) the date on which an offer (i.e. an offer to purchase shares in the company) becomes or is declared unconditional.

An additional disclosure requirement is set out in SSAP 23: *Accounting for Acquisitions and Mergers*, in that the effective date from which the results of major acquisitions have been brought into the accounts must be stated. This is relevant to the *acquisition method* of accounting for a business combination, described later in the chapter.

DISCLOSURE OF PRINCIPAL SUBSIDIARIES

The group accounts should contain the names of the principal subsidiaries, and an indication of the nature of their business. The proportion of the nominal value of the issued shares of each class held by the group should also be disclosed.

OUTSIDE OR MINORITY INTERESTS

Minority interests are defined in the ICMA's 'official terminology' as 'the shares held in a subsidiary company by members other than the holding company or its nominees plus the appropriate portion of the accumulated reserves (including share premium account)'. The standard requires them to be disclosed as a separate amount in the consolidated balance sheet, not as part of the shareholders' funds. Any *debit* balance relating to such interests should only be recognised if there is a binding obligation on minority shareholders to make good losses incurred which they are liable to meet.

The consolidated P&L account should disclose as separate items:

- the profits and losses attributable to outside interests, shown after arriving at group profit or loss after tax but before extraordinary items;
- minority interests in extraordinary items, to be shown as deductions from the relevant amounts.

RESTRICTIONS ON DISTRIBUTIONS

If there are significant restrictions on the ability of the holding company to distribute the retained profits of the group because of statutory, contractual or exchange control restrictions, the extent of the restrictions should be indicated.

SSAP 23: *ACCOUNTING FOR ACQUISITIONS AND MERGERS*

In the previous part of the chapter on SSAP 14: *Group Accounts*, the sections headed 'Changes in composition of the group' and 'Effective date of acquisition or disposal', referred to certain requirements in the event of subsidiaries being acquired or disposed. SSAP 23 gives details of the alternative accounting methods available for accounting for business combinations, those of *acquisition accounting* and *merger accounting*. The standard deals only with accounting in group accounts and not with the accounting to be used in individual companies' own accounts.

ACQUISITION ACCOUNTING

This is the traditional method of consolidation accounting, whereby the results of the acquired company are brought into the group accounts only from the date of acquisition. Assets acquired are stated at cost to the acquiring group.

MERGER ACCOUNTING

This method operates on the assumption that the combining companies have *always* been members of the same group, the justification being continuity of ownership. The full year's results are aggregated, even though the merger may have taken place part way through the year. Merger accounting is only permissible if specific conditions are met.

In merger accounting, it is not necessary to adjust the carrying values of the assets and liabilities of the subsidiary to fair value either in its own books or on consolidation. However, appropriate adjustments should be made to achieve uniformity of accounting policies between the combining companies.

When consolidating under the merger method, differences may arise if the carrying value of the investment in the subsidiary (i.e. the nominal value of shares issued plus the fair value of any additional consideration given) is greater or less than the nominal value of the shares being acquired. The difference is accounted for as follows:

(a) Where the carrying value of the investment is *less* than the nominal value of the shares acquired, the difference (credit balance) is treated as a non-distributable reserve arising on consolidation.

(b) Where the carrying value of the investment is *greater* than the nominal value of the shares acquired, the difference (debit balance) is treated as a capitalisation of reserves, which are reduced by an equivalent amount.

Conditions whereby merger accounting is permissible

The main criterion is whether or not the combination is based principally on a share for share exchange, as the following diagram shows:

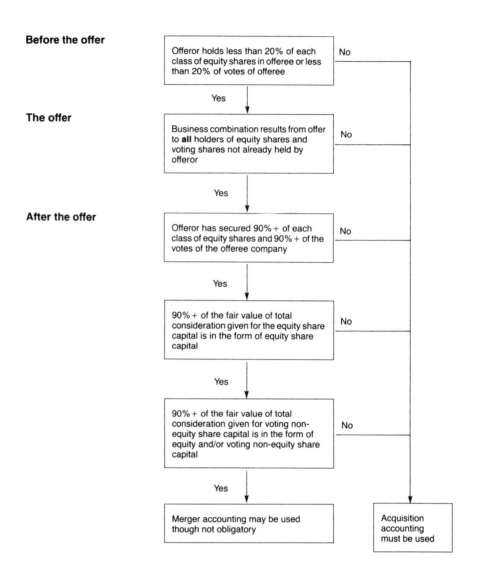

Before the offer

Offeror holds less than 20% of each class of equity shares in offeree or less than 20% of votes of offeree — No

Yes ↓

The offer

Business combination results from offer to **all** holders of equity shares and voting shares not already held by offeror — No

Yes ↓

After the offer

Offeror has secured 90% + of each class of equity shares and 90% + of the votes of the offeree company — No

Yes ↓

90% + of the fair value of total consideration given for the equity share capital is in the form of equity share capital — No

Yes ↓

90% + of the fair value of total consideration given for voting non-equity share capital is in the form of equity and/or voting non-equity share capital — No

Yes ↓

Merger accounting may be used though not obligatory

Acquisition accounting must be used

ACQUISITION ACCOUNTING AND MERGER ACCOUNTING CONTRASTED	Acquisition method	Merger method
Results of acquired company brought in from date of acquisition	√	X
Full year's results of both combining companies reflected in group accounts (i.e. as if the combining companies had 'always been together'), and corresponding figures adjusted.	X	√
Assets and liabilities in consolidated accounts at fair values (with increased depreciation charge as likely consequence)	√	X
Assets stated at cost to acquiring group	√	X
Goodwill calculated as per SSAP 22	√	X
Minority interests calculated	√	√
Reserve arising due to differences, e.g. when nominal value of shares issued exceeds aggregate of nominal value and reserves of other company	X	√
Uniformity of accounting policies to be achieved for combining companies	√	√

The decision as to whether acquisition or merger accounting is preferable depends upon the circumstances. The motive for adopting the merger method might be the desire to incorporate a whole year's profit of an acquired company to boost the distributable reserves of the acquiring company. However, there is no hard and fast rule, and each case should be considered on its merits.

DISCLOSURE REQUIREMENTS

The following matters should be disclosed in respect of all material business combinations, whether the acquisition or merger accounting method is used:

(a) the names of the combining companies;
(b) the number and class of the securities issued in respect of the combination, and details of any other consideration given;
(c) the accounting treatment adopted for the business combination (i.e. whether it has been accounted for as an acquisition or a merger); and
(d) the nature and amount of significant accounting adjustments by the combining companies to achieve consistency of accounting policies.

In respect of material *mergers*, the following information should be disclosed in the financial statements of the issuing company for the year in which the merger takes place:

(a) the fair value of the consideration given by the issuing company;

(b) an analysis of the current year's attributable profit before extraordinary items between that of before and after the effective date of the merger;

(c) an analysis of the attributable profit before extraordinary items of the current year up to the effective date of the merger and of the previous year between that of the issuing company and that of the subsidiary; and

(d) an analysis of extraordinary items so as to indicate whether each individual extraordinary item relates to pre- or post-merger events, and to which party to the merger the item relates.

APPLICABILITY OF STANDARD

The standard not only applies to business combinations where an existing company acquires another, but also to arrangements whereby a new holding company is formed and issues shares to the shareholders of two or more companies as consideration for the transfer to it of shares in both those companies. The example (Fig. 12.2) given in Section C: Useful Applied Materials of Storehouse plc's basis of presentation should be noted in this context.

C USEFUL APPLIED MATERIALS

The extracts shown in Fig. 12.1 are taken from the annual report of J. Sainsbury plc, and show that company's consolidated balance sheet and consolidated P&L account, and notes relevant to the treatment of subsidiaries and associates. The extract shown in Fig. 12.2 is from the annual report of Storehouse plc, showing the basis of presentation in respect of merger accounting provisions.

Figure 12.1 J. Sainsbury plc; consolidated accounts and notes

Balance Sheets
22nd March 1986

	Note	Group 1986 £m	Group 1985 £m	Company 1986 £m	Company 1985 £m
Fixed Assets					
Tangible Assets	1	1,069.3	876.2	993.3	816.6
Investments	2	55.6	48.8	91.1	80.6
		1,124.9	925.0	1,084.4	897.2
Current Assets					
Stocks		174.4	177.3	159.0	164.3
Debtors	5	37.4	27.4	35.4	26.0
ACT Recoverable	6	5.8	6.5	5.8	6.5
Cash at Bank and in Hand		48.6	37.2	46.8	35.9
		266.2	248.4	247.0	232.7
Creditors: due within one year	7	(643.5)	(578.4)	(615.9)	(562.4)
Net Current Liabilities		(377.3)	(330.0)	(368.9)	(329.7)
Total Assets Less Current Liabilities		747.6	595.0	715.5	567.5
Creditors: due after one year	8	(73.1)	(13.4)	(64.9)	(6.2)
Deferred Income	9	(13.6)	(17.8)	(13.6)	(17.8)
Minority Interest		(7.4)	(7.5)	—	—
		653.5	556.3	637.0	543.5
Capital and Reserves					
Called up Share Capital	10	175.3	174.2	175.3	174.2
Share Premium Account	11	12.0	5.6	12.0	5.6
Revaluation Reserve	12	31.9	34.0	31.9	34.0
Profit and Loss Account	13	434.3	342.5	417.8	329.7
		653.5	556.3	637.0	543.5

Group Profit and Loss Account
for the 52 weeks to 22nd March 1986

	Note	1986 £m	1985 £m
Group Sales (including VAT)		3,575.2	3,135.3
VAT		161.1	136.6
Group Sales (excluding VAT)		3,414.1	2,998.7
Cost of Sales		3,152.2	2,784.5
Gross Profit		261.9	214.2
Administrative Expenses		72.3	62.4
Other Operating Income (Net)	14	5.9	2.6
Net Interest (Payable)/Receivable	15	(0.6)	4.4
Retail Profit – net margin on VAT inclusive sales 5.45%(5.06%)	16	194.9	158.8
Associates – share of profit	4	13.6	9.7
Profit before Tax and Profit Sharing	17	208.5	168.5
Profit Sharing	17	15.8	12.1
Profit on Ordinary Activities before Tax		192.7	156.4
Tax on Profit on Ordinary Activities	20	65.4	48.0
Profit on Ordinary Activities after Tax		127.3	108.4
Minority Interest		0.1	(0.1)
Profit for Financial Year		127.4	108.3
Dividends	21	38.7	31.3
Profit Retained	13	88.7	77.0
Earnings per Share – actual		18.23p	15.61p
– fully taxed basis at 35%		17.92p	14.64p

Accounting Policies

Basis of Accounts The Group accounts, which have been prepared under the historical cost convention as modified by the revaluation of certain properties, consolidate the accounts of the Company and all its Subsidiaries made up to the Company's financial year-end. No Profit and Loss Account is presented for the Company as provided by Section 228(7) of the Companies Act 1985.

Associates Associates are those shown on page 24. An Associate is a company in which the Group participates in commercial and financial policy and has an interest of between 20 per cent. and 50 per cent. inclusive. Such companies are also related companies as defined in the Companies Act 1985.

Notes on the Accounts
at 22nd March 1986

2 Investments

	Group		Company	
	1986 £m	1985 £m	1986 £m	1985 £m
Subsidiaries (Note 3)	—	—	65.4	57.5
Associates (Note 4)	55.6	48.8	25.7	23.1
	55.6	48.8	91.1	80.6

3 Investment in Subsidiaries

	Share of Ordinary Allotted Capital
Homebase Limited	75%
J Sainsbury (Farms) Limited	100%
J. Sainsbury (Properties) Limited	100%
The Cheyne Investments Limited	100%
The Cheyne Investments Inc.	100%
J. Sainsbury Trustees Limited	Limited by guarantee
J Sainsbury Trustees (No. 2) Limited	100%
The Sainsbury Charitable Fund Limited	Limited by guarantee
Sainsbury's Business Training Centre Limited	100%

All Subsidiaries operate and are incorporated in the United Kingdom, with the exception of The Cheyne Investments Inc. which operates and is incorporated in the USA.

All shares are held by J Sainsbury plc, with the exception of The Cheyne Investments Inc., which is held by The Cheyne Investments Limited.

4 Investment in Associates

	Share of Allotted Capital	Share of Profit Before Tax	
		1986 £m	1985 £m
SavaCentre Limited	50%	6.3	4.8
16,180,050 "B" Ordinary Shares of £1 each			
Haverhill Meat Products Limited	50%	1.9	—
500,000 "B" Ordinary Shares of £1 each			
Breckland Farms Limited	50%	0.3	0.3
200,000 "B" Ordinary Shares of £1 each			
141,532 1% Redeemable Preference Shares of £1 each			
Kings Reach Investments Limited	28.76%	0.7	0.7
28,760 Ordinary Shares of 1p each			
Shaw's Supermarkets Inc.	21.27%	4.4	3.9
2,570,472 Common Capital Stock of $1 each			
		13.6	9.7

	Group £m	Company £m
Investments		
Balance 23rd March 1985	26.9	17.3
Currency movements	(2.1)	—
Balance 22nd March 1986	24.8	17.3
Share of Post Acquisition Reserves		
Balance 23rd March 1985	16.1	—
Currency movements	(0.9)	—
Share of retained profits for the year	7.2	—
Balance 22nd March 1986	22.4	—
Long Term Capital Advances		
Balance 23rd March 1985	5.8	5.8
Increase	2.6	2.6
Balance 22nd March 1986	8.4	8.4
Total Investment 22nd March 1986	55.6	25.7
23rd March 1985	48.8	23.1

The proportion of the profits of the Associates attributable to the Group and the reserves included in the Group balance sheet are taken from the audited accounts produced within three months of the balance sheet date, except Kings Reach Investments Limited where they are management accounts. The share of the results of Shaw's Supermarkets Inc. has been translated at the average rate of exchange for the relevant period. This method differs from that adopted in prior years, but no restatement has been made as the effect is immaterial.

The reserves shown above are after deducting dividends received by J Sainsbury plc of £0.5 million (1985 nil) and by The Cheyne Investments Inc. of £0.1 million (1985 £0.1 million).

All Associates operate and are incorporated in the United Kingdom with the exception of Shaw's Supermarkets Inc. which operates and is incorporated in the USA.

5 Debtors

	Group	
	1986	1985
	£m	£m
Trade	1.3	1.4
Amounts owed by Associates	5.0	3.0
Other Debtors	29.8	17.8
Prepayments	1.3	5.2
	37.4	27.4

20 Tax on Profit on Ordinary Activities

	Group	
	1986	1985
	£m	£m
The tax charge for the year is:		
Corporation tax	57.1	43.6
Deferred tax	2.6	1.0
Share of Associates' tax	5.7	3.4
	65.4	48.0

Figure 12.2 Storehouse plc; merger accounting

NOTES TO THE ACCOUNTS

1 BASIS OF PRESENTATION

The Company was incorporated on 26 September 1985 and commenced trading on 6 January 1986. Therefore, no comparative figures are available for the Company.

Offers were made by the Company to acquire all the issued ordinary shares and the convertible unsecured loan stock of BHS and Habitat Mothercare. The offers for the ordinary shares were declared unconditional in all respects on 6 January 1986. As at 29 March 1986, the Company owned 93.5% of BHS and 96.6% of Habitat Mothercare. On 16 May 1986, the Company compulsorily acquired the minority interests in these companies which have been treated as wholly-owned subsidiaries in these accounts.

The accounts of BHS and Habitat Mothercare and their subsidiaries have been consolidated in accordance with the principles of merger accounting. The Consolidated Profit and Loss Account therefore combines the results of these companies for the 52 weeks ended 29 March 1986. The comparative figures combine the results of BHS for the 52 weeks ended 30 March 1985 and of Habitat Mothercare for the 53 weeks ended 31 March 1985. The comparative Consolidated Balance Sheet is presented as if the merger had been in effect as at the end of March 1985.

The Company has adopted the merger relief provisions of the Companies Act 1985 and has recorded the carrying value of its investment in BHS and Habitat Mothercare at the nominal value of the shares issued as consideration together with related expenses. The excess of the nominal value of the shares acquired over the carrying value of the investment has been credited to other reserves on consolidation.

No adjustments have been made to the carrying value of the assets and liabilities of BHS and Habitat Mothercare except for those adjustments necessary to achieve uniformity of accounting policies (see Note 19).

1

(a) What criteria does SSAP 1 *Accounting for Associated Companies* (revised April 1982) state should be used when considering whether a company should be accounted for as an associated company of an investing company?

(10 marks)

(b) How should a holding company treat the following items in the financial statements of an associated company, when preparing group accounts?
(i) turnover;
(ii) extraordinary items;
(iii) inter-company profits;
(iv) goodwill.

(10 marks)
(20 marks)

(Chartered Association of Certified Accountants, June 1984)

2 As a result of sections 36–40 of the Companies Act 1981 the merger ('pooling of interest') method of accounting is permissible in certain circumstances instead of the traditional acquisition ('purchase') method and by using the merger method a different distribution of profits policy may be available to the group.

For purposes of illustration of the two methods, suppose that one share of Company X is offered for one share of Company Y and the offer is accepted. Also assume at the time of the merger a share of Y is valued at £7 and the fair value of Y's net assets is £650 000 being a decrease of £30 000 in fixed assets and £20 000 working capital. The balance sheets of X and Y immediately prior to the merger are as follows:

	X (£000)	Y (£000)
Fixed assets	1 100	700
Current assets	300	100
	1 400	800
Creditors	400	200
	1 000	600
Share capital (ordinary £1 shares)	700	100
Capital reserve	70	
Revenue reserves	230	500
	1 000	600

Required:
(a) identify the circumstances in which the merger method of accounting is permissible; (4 marks)

(b) draw up summarised consolidated balance sheets immediately after the merger, using each of the two methods of accounting for consolidations, and (10 marks)

(c) contrast the two consolidated balance sheets evaluating the consequences and effectiveness of each method of accounting. (8 marks)

Your working sheets must be submitted (Total 22 marks)

(Institute of Chartered Secretaries and Administrators, 1986)

E ANSWERS

1(a) This topic is covered in detail in the first part of the chapter.

1(b)

(i) The investing group should not include its share of the associate company's turnover with that of the group. However, if the amount is so material in the context of the group that more detailed information would assist in giving a true and fair view, then a note should be given which discloses the total turnover.

(ii) If extraordinary items of the associated company would be regarded as extraordinary in the context of the investing group's results, then the share of such items should be disclosed separately from extraordinary items arising from companies belonging to the group.

(iii) Inter-company profits which are material and unrealised should be eliminated, whether they arise in the investing company or the associate.

(iv) The investing company's share of any goodwill in the associated company should be disclosed in the balance sheet of the group.

2(a) This topic is covered in detail in the section of the chapter on SSAP 23.

2(b)

Acquisition method

X Ltd Consolidated Balance Sheet

		£000
Fixed assets (1 100 + 670)		1 770
Goodwill		150
		1 920
Current assets (300 + 80)	380	
Creditors (400 + 200)	(600)	
	—	(220)
		1 700
Share capital (700 + 100)		800
Capital reserves (70 + 600)		670
Revenue reserves		230
		1 700

Workings:
(a) Goodwill:
   Value of consideration given 100 000 shares @
      £7 each

	700 000
Assets and liabilities acquired, at fair value	
	550 000
	150 000

(b) Share premium:
   Value of consideration, as above   700 000
   Less: Nominal value of shares issued   100 000

                                   600 000

Merger Method

X Ltd Consolidated Balance Sheet

Fixed assets (1 100 + 700)	1 800
Current assets (300 + 100)	400
	2 200
Creditors (400 + 200)	(600)
	1 600
Share capital (700 + 100*)	800
Capital reserve	70
Revenue reserves (230 + 500)	730
	1 600

*i.e. X's original share capital plus the 100 000 shares issued for Y.

2(c) The major consequence of adopting the merger method of accounting has been to increase the amount of distributable reserves when compared with those arising under the acquisition method. This is of obvious benefit to the existing (and new) shareholders of X Ltd, as under the acquisition method, pre-acquisition profits are not available for dividend.

    The statement of standard accounting practice, SSAP 23, lays down detailed criteria for determining whether the merger method can be applied, and this acts as a safeguard for the interests of creditors of the companies being merged. The argument against merger accounting that it creates 'instant distributable reserves' is counterbalanced by the fact that the combined total is no higher than that of the distributable reserves of the individual companies immediately prior to the merger.

F A STEP FURTHER

The following references are given for the purpose of further study:

H. K. Jaeger, *The Structure of Consolidated Accounting* (Macmillan).
Selected Accounting Standards – Interpretation Problems Explained
(ICAEW), pp. 95–140, 255–300.
P. A. Holgate, *Accountants Digest No. 189 – SSAP 23: Accounting for
acquisitions and mergers* (ICAEW).
Financial Reporting 1983–84 (ICAEW), pp. 87–106.

Chapter 13

Foreign currency translation

SSAP 20

A GETTING STARTED

If this book were purchased in the UK, the payment would have been made in pounds sterling. In other countries where this book is available, the payment would be made in the local currency, for example, Hong Kong or Singaporean dollars, or Sri Lankan rupees. Whatever the currency, the company which publishes the book has to make appropriate accounting entries in its records in its own local currency, and has to cope with the various problems of fluctuating exchange rates and asset and liability balances held by foreign subsidiaries which are denominated in foreign currencies.

SSAP 20 addresses itself to these problems, and explains methods to be adopted both by individual companies and groups of companies for the purpose of foreign currency translation. The standard is complex, and one author estimated recently that it contains over 3 000 alternative accounting possibilities. Examination questions are unlikely to require a knowledge of all of these!

B ESSENTIAL PRINCIPLES

The explanatory note to the standard sets out the objectives of foreign currency translation as follows:

'The translation of foreign currency transactions and financial statements should produce results which are generally compatible with the effects of rate changes on a company's cash flows and its equity and should ensure that the financial statements present a true and fair view of the results of management actions. Consolidated statements should reflect the financial results and relationships as measured in the foreign currency financial statements prior to translation.'

The standard itself is split into two main areas:

1. The individual company stage, whereby a company may enter directly into business transactions denominated in foreign currencies, and may have asset and liability balances which also are so denominated; and
2. The consolidated financial statements stage, whereby the results of foreign subsidiaries must be incorporated within the consolidated results of the group.

1 THE INDIVIDUAL COMPANY STAGE

use FX at date of transaction Except: contracted rate forward contract

Individual transactions: the exchange rate in operation on the date on which the transaction occurred should be used. If rates of exchange are fairly stable, however, an average rate for a period may be used.

If certain transactions are to be settled at a rate specified in a contract, or are covered by a related or matching forward contract, then the 'contracted rate' should be used. *↳ say*

The standard gives specific advice with regard to 'non-monetary' assets and 'monetary' assets and liabilities denominated in foreign currencies, as detailed under the headings below.

Non-monetary assets (e.g. plant, machinery and equity investments)

Once translated and recorded in the company's local currency,* no subsequent translations will normally be made. The exception to this is where such assets have been financed by borrowings in foreign currencies, in which case, subject to certain conditions explained later in the chapter, the amounts are translated at the end of each accounting period at the closing rates of exchange.

*Defined as the currency of the primary economic environment in which it operates and generates cash flows.

Monetary assets (e.g. cash and bank balances, amounts receivable and payable)

These should be translated according to the rates of exchange ruling at the balance sheet date, unless there are related or matching forward contracts, in which case the 'contracted' rate is used.

Exchange gains or losses

These arise primarily in situations where the rate prevailing at the time that a transaction is recorded differs from that used when the transaction is settled. Such gains or losses should be included in the profit or loss on ordinary activities unless they arise from 'extraordinary' events (see SSAP 6), in which case they are included as part of such items.

In the case of exchange gains relating to long-term monetary items (e.g. long-dated foreign loans), the prudence concept must be taken into consideration when deciding whether to incorporate all or part of such gains in circumstances where there are doubts as to the convertibility or marketability of the currency in question.

Gains or losses arising from group inter-company transactions should be reported within the individual company's P&L account, in the same way as third party transactions.

SUMMARY

Individual Company (main provisions only)

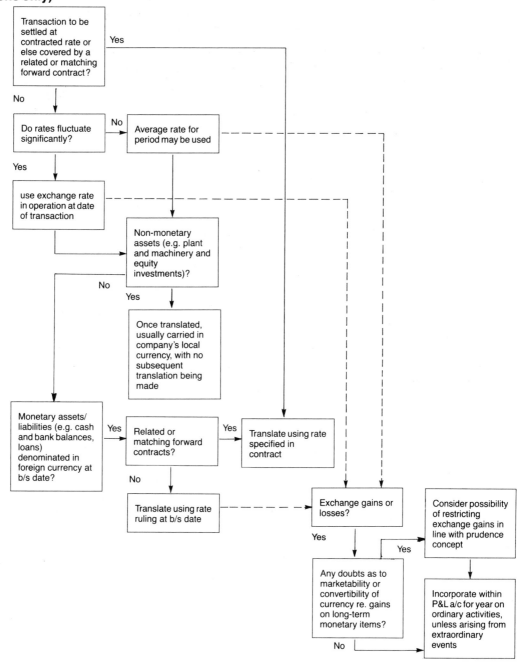

2 THE CONSOLIDATED FINANCIAL STATEMENTS STAGE

b/s date

Two methods are considered for the purpose of translating financial statements for consolidation purposes; the *closing rate/net investment* method, and the *temporal* method. The method chosen (usually the former) should reflect the financial and other operational relationships which exist between an investing company and its foreign enterprises.

The Closing Rate/Net Investment Method

i) not individual assets but overall investment

Under this method, the balance sheet amounts in the foreign subsidiary are translated using the rate of exchange ruling at the balance sheet date (i.e. the 'closing rate'). This method is based on the 'net investment' concept whereby it is not the value of the individual assets and liabilities which is relevant, but the value of the overall net investment in the subsidiary. Any difference which arises if the closing rate differs from that ruling at the previous balance sheet date (or at the date of any subsequent capital injection or reduction) should be adjusted on reserves.

Profit and loss account items

The standard allows either the closing rate or an average rate to be applied to P&L a/c, giving the following arguments.

Closing rate: more likely to achieve objective of translation (see p. 165)

Average rate:* reflects more fairly the profits or losses and cash flows as they arise to the group throughout the accounting period.

Once the rate is chosen it should be applied consistently in future accounting periods. Where the average rate differs from the closing rate, a difference will arise which should be adjusted on reserves.

*'Calculated by the method considered most appropriate for the circumstances of the foreign enterprise.'

The Temporal Method

Whilst most foreign operations are carried out by organisations which operate as virtually autonomous entities, there are occasions where the foreign trade is conducted as a direct extension of the trade of the investing company, and the results of the foreign enterprise are regarded as being more dependent upon the economic environment of the investing company's local currency than on its own reporting currency.

In such cases, the 'net investment' concept is regarded as inappropriate, and the transactions of the foreign enterprise are treated as though they had been made by the investing company itself in its own currency, being translated by means of the 'temporal' method. The temporal method is identical with that used at the individual company stage described earlier in the chapter.

The decision as to whether the temporal method is appropriate hinges upon the relative dominance of the investing company's 'economic environment'. The explanatory note to the standard gives the following list of factors to be taken into account when arriving at the decision:

(a) the extent to which the cash flows of the enterprise have a direct impact upon those of the investing company;

(b) the extent to which the functioning of the enterprise is dependent directly upon the investing company;

(c) the currency in which the majority of the trading transactions are denominated;

(d) the major currency to which the operation is exposed in its financing structure.

Additionally, it gives three specific circumstances where the temporal method may be appropriate, where the foreign enterprise:

(i) acts as a selling agency receiving stocks of goods from the investing company and remits the proceeds back to the company;

(ii) produces a raw material or manufactures parts or subassemblies which are then shipped to the investing company for inclusion in its own products;

(iii) is located overseas for tax, exchange control or similar reasons to act as a means of raising finance for other companies in the group.

Foreign branches

The translation method to be used depends upon the degree of autonomy which the branch enjoys:

High degree of autonomy: Closing rate/net investment method

Extension of company's trade, and cash flows have direct impact on those of company: Temporal method

AREAS OF HYPERINFLATION

In certain countries, a very high rate of inflation exists, which serves to distort any translation of accounts produced under the historical cost concept. In such circumstances, appropriate adjustments should be made to the financial statements to reflect current price levels before the translation process takes place.

COMPANIES COVERED AGAINST EXCHANGE RATE FLUCTUATIONS

In the previous parts of this section, it has been seen how exchange gains and losses are normally incorporated within the company's P&L arising from ordinary activities. In many cases, companies enter into currency hedging arrangements by borrowing foreign currency to cushion them from any adverse effects arising from exchange rate movements. Where this cover exists, and subject to certain conditions, the standard regards it as being inappropriate to record an accounting profit or loss when exchange rates change, and requires exchange adjustments to be taken directly to reserves. It also allows the 'closing rate' to be applied to the company's equity investments, as opposed to carrying forward the original translated amounts. The conditions are:

(a) in any accounting period, exchange gains or losses arising on the borrowings may be offset only to the extent of exchange differences arising on the equity investments;

(b) the foreign currency borrowings, whose exchange gains or losses are used in the offset process, should not exceed, in aggregate, the total amount of cash that the investments are expected to be able to generate, whether from profits or otherwise; and

(c) the accounting treatment adopted should be applied consistently from period to period.

Similar provisions apply where a group has used foreign borrowings to finance group investments in a foreign enterprise or to provide a hedge against exchange risks applying to similar existing investments. One additional condition is, however, laid down in such circumstances:

(d) the relationship between the investing company and the foreign enterprises concerned should be such as to justify the use of the closing rate method for consolidation purposes.

DISCLOSURE REQUIREMENTS

The following information should be disclosed in the financial statements with regard to foreign currency translation:

1. The translation methods used;
2. The treatment accorded to exchange differences;
3. The net amount of exchange gains and losses on foreign currency borrowings;
4. The net movement on reserves arising from exchange differences.

Consolidated financial statements (main provisions only)

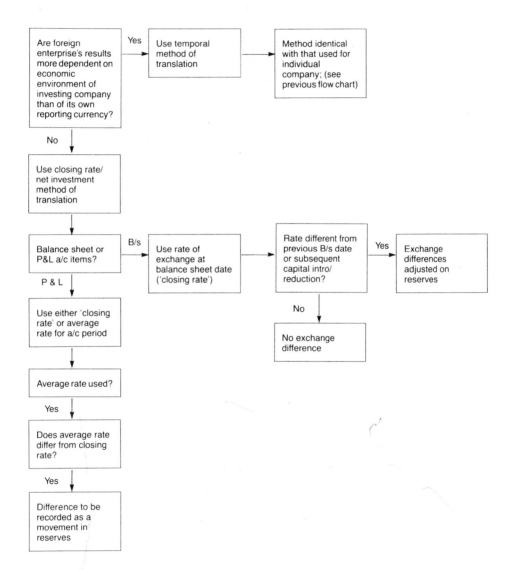

C USEFUL APPLIED MATERIALS

The following extracts (Figs 13.1 and 13.2) from the published accounts of UK public limited companies have been chosen to illustrate the accounting treatment adopted towards the translation of foreign currency.

Figure 13.1 The Boots Company plc; treatment of foreign currencies

Foreign currencies

The results of overseas companies are translated into sterling on an average exchange rate basis, weighted by the actual results of each month.

Assets and liabilities of overseas subsidiaries are translated into sterling at the rates of exchange ruling at the date of the group balance sheet.

All translation differences are taken to reserves. Other exchange gains or losses are taken to trading profit where they relate to items of a trading nature. Overseas investments are stated at the rate of exchange in force at the date each investment was made.

Figure 13.2 Foseco Minsep plc; treatment of foreign currencies

Foreign currencies

Company: Assets and liabilities denominated in foreign currencies are translated at the rate of exchange ruling at the balance sheet date. Transactions in foreign currencies are recorded at the rate ruling at the date of the transactions. All differences are taken to the profit and loss account.

Group: the accounts of overseas subsidiaries are translated at the rate of exchange ruling at the balance sheet date with the exception of the year's profit and loss account which is translated at the average of the mid-month exchange rates in the year. The exchange differences arising on the retranslation of opening net assets and on the retranslation of the profit and loss account to closing rates of exchange are taken directly to reserves. All other translation differences are taken to the profit and loss account with the exception of differences on foreign currency borrowings to the extent that they are to finance or provide a hedge against Group equity investments in foreign enterprises which are taken directly to reserves.

D RECENT EXAMINATION QUESTIONS

1   With regard to SSAP 20 *Foreign Currency Translation*:

   (a) Explain the closing rate/net investment method.   (7 marks)
   (b) Explain the temporal method.   (7 marks)

(c) What factors should be taken into account in deciding whether the temporal method should be adopted? Give TWO examples of situations where this method may be the most appropriate.

(11 marks)

(25 marks)

(Chartered Association of Certified Accountants, June 1985)

2

(a) Outline the TWO major methods of accounting for foreign currency translation, explaining clearly the objectives upon which they are based. (12 marks)

(b) Should exchange differences appear in the profit and loss account or be charged direct to reserves? State the reasons for your answer. (8 marks)

(20 marks)

(Chartered Association of Certified Accountants, June 1986)

3 Home Ltd is incorporated in the UK and rents mobile homes to holidaymakers in this country and in Carea. The company has a head office in London and a branch in Carea where the local currency is 'mics'. The following balances are extracted from the books of the head office and its 'self-accounting' branch at 31 December 1984.

	Head office (£)	Branch (Mics)
Debit balances		
Fixed assets at cost	450 000	900 000
Debtors and cash	17 600	36 000
Operating costs	103 700	225 000
Branch current account	42 600	—
	613 900	1 161 000
Credit balances		
Share capital	200 000	—
Retained profit, 1 January 1984	110 800	—
Sales revenue	186 300	480 000
Creditors	9 700	25 000
Head office current account	—	420 000
Accumulated depreciation	107 100	236 000
	613 900	1 161 000

The following information is provided regarding exchange rates, some of which is relevant.

The fixed assets of the branch were acquired when there were 8 mics to the £. Exchange rates ruling during 1984 were:

	Mics to the £
1 January	6
Average	5
31 December	4

There are no cash or goods in transit between head office and branch at the year end.

Required:
The final accounts of Home Ltd for 1984. The accounts should be expressed in £s sterling and, for this purpose, the conversion of mics should be made in accordance with the temporal method of translation as specified in SSAP 20 entitled *Foreign Currency Translation*. (24 marks)

(Institute of Chartered Secretaries and Administrators, Dec. 1985)

E ANSWERS

1(a) Under the closing rate/net investment method of foreign currency translation, the balance sheet amounts in the foreign subsidiary are translated using the rate of exchange ruling at the balance sheet date (i.e. the 'closing rate'), with the exception of equity capital, which is translated at the rate when acquired. Profit and loss account items are translated at either the closing rate or the average rate for the year. This method is based on the 'net investment' concept whereby it is not the value of the individual assets and liabilities which is relevant, but the value of the overall net investment in the subsidiary. The objective of consolidation is to present information which is useful to decision-makers in the parent company's country, but without necessarily presenting the results as though the parent company and its subsidiaries were a single entity.

1(b) Whilst most foreign operations are carried out by organisations which operate as virtually autonomous entities, there are occasions where the foreign trade is conducted as a direct extension of the trade of the investing company, and the results of the foreign enterprise are regarded as being more dependent upon the economic environment of the investing (i.e. parent) company's local currency than on its own reporting currency.

In such cases, the 'net investment' concept (upon which the 'closing rate' method of foreign currency translation is based) is regarded as inappropriate, and the transactions of the foreign enterprise are treated as though they had been made by the investing company itself in its own currency, being translated by means of the 'temporal' method. The temporal method is therefore based on the premiss that the objective of consolidation is to present the results of the parent company and its subsidiaries as though it was a single entity.

Under the temporal method, monetary assets, current liabilities and long-term liabilities are translated at the rate of exchange prevailing at the end of the year, but non-monetary assets and depreciation are translated at the exchange rate at the date of purchase. Equity capital is translated at the exchange rate when acquired. Profit and loss account items are translated at the average rate for the year.

1(c) The decision as to whether the temporal method is appropriate hinges upon the relative dominance of the investing company's 'economic environment'. The explanatory note to the standard gives the following list of factors to be taken into account when arriving at the decision:

(a) the extent to which the cash flows of the enterprise have a direct impact upon those of the investing company;
(b) the extent to which the functioning of the enterprise is dependent directly upon the investing company;
(c) the currency in which the majority of the trading transactions are denominated;
(d) the major currency to which the operation is exposed in its financing structure.

Two examples of circumstances where the temporal method may be appropriate are where the foreign enterprise:

(i) acts as a selling agency receiving stocks of goods from the investing company and remits the proceeds back to the company;
(ii) produces a raw material or manufactures parts or subassemblies which are then shipped to the investing company for inclusion in its own products.

2(a) See answer to **1(a)** and **(b)** above.

2(b) For individual companies, exchange gains or losses arise primarily in situations where the rate prevailing at the time that a transaction is recorded differs from that used when the transaction is settled. Such gains or losses should be included in the P&L account as part of the profit or loss on ordinary activities unless they arise from 'extraordinary' events (see SSAP 6), in which case they are included as part of such items.

In the case of exchange gains relating to long-term monetary items (e.g. long-dated foreign loans), the prudence concept must be taken into consideration when deciding whether to incorporate all or part of such gains in circumstances where there are doubts as to the convertibility or marketability of the currency in question.

Gains or losses arising from group inter-company transactions should be reported within the individual company's P&L account, in the same way as third party transactions.

For consolidation purposes, exchange gains or losses are adjusted directly on reserves.

3 Using the temporal method of foreign currency translation, the trial balance of the Carea branch is as follows:

	Mics	Rate	Debit(£)	Credit(£)
Fixed assets at cost	900 000	8	112 500	
Debtors and cash	36 000	4	9 000	
Operating costs	225 000	5	45 000	
Difference on exchange*			7 850	
Sales revenue	480 000	5		96 000
Creditors	25 000	4		6 250
Head office current account	420 000	Actual		42 600
Accumulated depreciation	236 000	8		29 500
			174 350	174 350

*Balancing figure.

The final accounts of Home Ltd for 1984 are as follows:

Profit and Loss Account for the Year ended 31 December 1984

		£
Sales revenue (186 300 + 96 000)		282 300
Operating costs (103 700 + 45 000)	148 700	
Exchange losses	7 850	
		156 550
Net profit		125 750

Balance Sheet as at 31 December 1984

Fixed assets, at cost (450 000 + 112 500)	562 500	
Less: Depreciation (107 100 + 29 500)	136 600	
		425 900
Debtors and cash (17 600 + 9 000)	26 600	
Less: Creditors (9 700 + 6 250)	15 950	
		10 650
		436 550
Share capital		200 000
Retained reserves (110 800 + 125 750)		236 550
		436 550

F A STEP FURTHER

The following references are given for the purpose of further study:

C. Westwick, *Accounting for Overseas Operations* (Gower).
Selected Accounting Standards – Interpretation Problems Explained
(ICAEW), pp. 201–54.
Financial Reporting 1983–84 (ICAEW), pp. 65–85.

Inflation accounting

SSAP 16

The mandatory status of SSAP 16 entitled *Current Cost Accounting* was suspended in June 1985, largely as a result of widespread non-compliance by the companies to whom it applied. The standard had the intention of requiring listed companies and certain other large entities to provide *current cost information* in addition to the conventional historical cost information.

From an examinee's viewpoint, it is unlikely that questions will be set which require a detailed knowledge of the contents of SSAP 16. Instead, an awareness of the main principles of 'inflation accounting' is necessary, together with an understanding of the reasons for the abandonment of the mandatory status of the standard. The following should therefore be seen as a guide in outline only, and reference should be made to one or more of the texts mentioned in 'A Step Further' at the end of this appendix.

SSAP 2, *Disclosure of Accounting Policies*, requires companies, *inter alia*, to disclose specific accounting policies adopted when preparing the financial statements. The first of these policies is usually a statement that the accounts have been prepared 'under the historical cost convention, as modified by the revaluation of certain land and buildings'.

Historical cost accounting (HCA) is the traditional method of accounting whereby all items are recorded at their purchase price at the date of acquisition. HCA has several advantages, including:

- it provides a degree of objectivity, as measurements are based on actual costs;
- it is the only system of accounting recognised for the purpose of taxation assessment in the UK;
- it is compatible with the double-entry bookkeeping system;
- verification by auditors is relatively straightforward;
- it is easy to understand by both accountants and users.

However, HCA has disadvantages, which are alluded to in the addition of the words 'as modified by the revaluation of certain land and buildings' in the note on accounting policies mentioned earlier. If HCA is such a reliable system, why should it need 'modifying'? The answer is that despite its advantages, the use of HCA can paint a misleading picture of the results of a business because of its inability to reflect the distorting effects of *inflation*.

Over a period of years, inflation results in a decline in the purchasing power of money, with the result that:

- fixed assets and stock cost more to replace than their original cost;
- assets such as debtors lose value, as debtors are able to use 'devalued' currency to pay their debts. Creditors and other liabilities lose value for the same reason;
- it becomes difficult to compare the financial statements of one period with those of another, due to differences in the relative values of amounts appearing within the statements;
- profits are overstated when using HCA, as inadequate provision is made for the future replacement prices of fixed assets and stock;
- asset values are understated due to their inclusion at their historical cost rather than their current value at the balance sheet date. However, as we have seen, HCA is frequently modified to the extent of allowing revaluations of certain fixed assets, notably land and buildings.

The use of HCA may lead to companies paying excess dividends and agreeing over-generous pay settlements with employees, on the basis of inflated profits. In addition, analysis of the company's performance is likely to be distorted, and problems lie in store for the company when they come to replace fixed assets at current prices, without having ensured adequate retention of profits for that purpose.

If it is acknowledged that HCA is an imperfect system, one would suppose that suitable alternatives exist to overcome the deficiencies. The accountancy profession has, for nearly two decades, attempted to find the answer in the form primarily of *Current Purchasing Power Accounting* (CPP) and *Current Cost Accounting* (CCA), and SSAPs have been issued and subsequently withdrawn on each. At present, as explained earlier, SSAP 16, *Current Cost Accounting*, does not have mandatory status. In practice, this means that hardly any companies will be willing to meet the considerable expense in terms of both time and money required to comply with the standard.

Although the whole question of inflation accounting is in a state of limbo at the time of writing, it is not impossible that the profession may yet again pick up the pieces and try and attain a solution which is simple, workable, inexpensive to operate and acceptable to both preparers and users of the information. Both CPP and CCA have their protagonists within the accountancy profession, but company directors must be convinced that, whatever method is decided upon, it represents a useful guide to policy-making, and the advantages outweigh the costs.

There follows a brief explanation of both CPP and CCA accounting.

CURRENT PURCHASING POWER ACCOUNTING

This is based on the translation of the amounts appearing in the historical cost accounts into inflation adjusted values by the use of 'CPP units', which represent stable monetary units calculated by reference to general price indices. Debtors and creditors, which represent actual amounts receivable or payable, would not be converted, nor would cash and bank balances.

Advantages claimed for CPP are that it provides a 'real' measure of profit, and allows meaningful comparisons to be made from one year to the next. The system is based on HCA, and therefore retains the advantages of that system as listed previously. Disadvantages of CPP are that the application of general price indices in the calculation of CPP units could distort the results of specific enterprises. There may also be difficulties in obtaining the acceptance of users to the concept of an artificial currency designed exclusively for accounting.

CURRENT COST ACCOUNTING

SSAP 16 requires that public limited companies and certain other large companies should present CCA accounting statements in addition to the HC accounts. These comprise:

(a) A **CC profit and loss account**, whereby the net profit or loss as calculated in the HC accounts is subject to adjustments which show the increased costs required to maintain the *operating capability* of the business, i.e. the ability of the business to maintain the output of goods and services from its existing resources. The adjustments are as follows:

  (i)   The depreciation adjustment, which shows the extra depreciation that is required to provide for the *replacement cost of fixed assets*, rather than the original, historic cost.
  (ii) The cost of sales adjustment, which reflects the difference between the historical cost of stock sold and its replacement cost.
  (iii) The monetary working capital adjustment, which is a calculation of the extra finance required to fund the increased net debtors (debtors less creditors)* which are likely to result when inflation raises invoice prices.
  (iv) The gearing adjustment, which is applied as a percentage reduction to the total of the previous three adjustments. It recognises that many companies are part financed by outside

* Where the company has net trade *creditors*, the effect of the monetary working capital adjustment may be to reduce the necessary cost of sales adjustment.

borrowing, and that the external financiers should carry an appropriate part of the burden of inflation which falls upon the company.

(b) A **CC balance sheet**, which shows fixed assets and stock at replacement prices, which may be calculated by reference to price indices. A current cost reserve records the surpluses or deficits caused by the changes to the historical cost figures, both in the P&L account and the balance sheet. No amendments are made to actual amounts owed or owing, such as debtors and creditors, nor to cash and bank balances.

A STEP FURTHER

The following references are given for the purpose of further study:

G. Whittington, *Inflation Accounting – an Introduction to the Debate* (Cambridge University Press).
P. Clayton and J. Blake, *Inflation Accounting* (Longman Professional).
'Accounting for the effects of changing prices: a Handbook' (Accounting Standards Committee).